LIMITS UNLEASHED

A CONVERSATION BETWEEN YOU AND YOUR INNER SELF

ALVIN KALICHARAN

Your only limits are those you set yourself!

Unlock your potential and change lives—all proceeds from this book go directly to charity. Make a difference today!

INDIA • SINGAPORE • MALAYSIA

ISBN
Hardcase 979-8-89673-786-5
Paperback 979-8-89588-920-6

DEDICATION

To my lovely wife, Sugandha, whose spirit embodies the essence of freedom and boundless possibilities.

To my daughter, Anusha, whose presence signifies a new beginning and the promise of a brighter tomorrow.

To my daughter, Aahana, whose compassion and warmth inspire every page of this journey. Your love and strength are the heart of this book.

Table of Contents

Preface

In a world where everyone chases the same dream—happiness, success, wealth, health, lifelong friendships, liberation, and lasting love—the path to true fulfilment often feels just out of reach. We all start with similar physical abilities and resources. Yet, only a rare few rise above the rest. These are the exceptional individuals you can count on one hand. They go on to rule the world, achieve unparalleled heights, and live truly fulfilled lives. Why is that? Why do so many find themselves trapped by their circumstances, unable to unlock the vast potential within?

What if the key to an extraordinary life doesn't lie in your external circumstances, but within you? What if the limits you believe in are nothing more than illusions waiting to be shattered?

Life's journey is filled with twists, turns, and endless possibilities. While countless philosophies claim to offer the path to greatness, what if there were a practical framework that shows you how to live up to your fullest potential?

Within the pages of *Limits Unleashed*, you'll meet a boy from a small town where the horizon seemed distant—until he awakened to the limitless power within him through the LIMIT Framework.

Part I of the book takes you on a transformative journey. It challenges everything you thought you knew about yourself and the world around you. It pushes boundaries, encouraging you to think beyond limitations. It reshapes your perceptions, opening your mind to new possibilities. Most importantly, it uncovers the untapped potential that lies within each of us.

Part II encourages you to take a step back and reflect on your journey so far. It asks you to assess how aligned you are with your true self—how close or far you might be. This isn't just about going through the motions of life. It's about discovering and unlocking the boundless potential that lies within you.

Are you ready to break free from the constraints of your environment, tap into your inner strength, and embark on a path that only the truly unstoppable can follow? The journey to your best self begins here. Will you take the first step?

Acknowledgements

To my dearest mom, Asha, the woman who gave me life and has always been my greatest support—this book is a testament to your unwavering love and prayers. You brought me into this world, nurtured me with your boundless care, and believed in me even when I doubted myself. Your constant prayers for my well-being and success have been my guiding light, giving me strength when I needed it most. Every step I take is a reflection of the sacrifices you've made and the love you've poured into my life. For that, and for everything, I am forever grateful. This book is as much yours as it is mine.

A special thanks to my sister, Aruna, whose endless support, unwavering motivation, and steadfast belief in my ability to write this book have been a driving force. Your encouragement has made this endeavour possible, and I am deeply grateful for your presence in my life.

I extend my heartfelt gratitude to everyone who has contributed to my journey of learning and growth. Your insights, experiences, and support have been invaluable.

From Me to You!

For the Young Dreamers

Discover Your Superpowers: I encourage you to explore the amazing potential that lies within you. As you journey through this book, you'll uncover your unique strengths and learn that, with the right mindset, you can overcome any challenge and grow stronger every day. We all have incredible abilities waiting to be discovered, and I'm here to guide you as you find your own superpowers. Let's embark on this exciting adventure together and see just how powerful you really are!

For the Explorers

Break Boundaries, Build Dreams: I'm here to remind you that the only limits are the ones you set for yourself. This book is all about motivating you to push past what you think is possible, break through barriers, and dream bigger than ever before. Whether you're a teenager or a young adult, remember this: With determination, you can tackle any challenge. With creativity, you can find solutions to even the toughest problems. And with a fearless mindset, no obstacle is too great to overcome. Your future is in your hands, and I'm here to help you build it—one dream at a time.

For the Wise and Experienced

Redefining Possibilities at Every Stage of Life: I invite you to embrace the idea that growth and discovery are not confined to youth. This book is for those in midlife and beyond who are ready to challenge the limits they've accepted and explore new possibilities with confidence and curiosity. Life is a journey of continuous evolution, and no matter where you are on that path, there are still dreams to be realised, skills to be honed, and adventures to embark upon. Together, let's redefine what's possible at every stage of life, proving that it's never too late to grow, discover, and thrive.

For Everyone

Embrace the Power Within: This is an invitation for you to discover the incredible strength that lies within, no matter your age or stage of life. By understanding and pushing past the limits you've set for yourself, you can unlock new potential and lead a more fulfilling life. This book is about recognising your boundaries, then finding the courage and creativity to transcend them. Whether you're just beginning your journey or well along the path, the message is clear: the power to grow, change, and achieve is already inside you. All you have to do is embrace it.

Read and Heed!

As you journey through the pages of this book, I encourage you to keep a pen and paper close by. Self-reflection is key to unlocking the transformative power of the action items in each chapter.

Whether you are a young dreamer, eager to discover your path, an explorer, searching for new possibilities, or someone wise and experienced, seeking deeper meaning, these exercises are for you. They will help you connect with your inner self, align with your true purpose, and embrace the incredible power that lies within you.

This book will help you find your "Why" and "What," while leaving the "How" up to you. Your journey is uniquely yours. The insights you gain, the emotions you feel, and the realizations you come to will guide you in discovering your "How" and working toward a life filled with purpose, meaning, and fulfilment. You'll have the freedom to determine what works for you and learn how to apply the LIMIT Framework in your own life to unleash your potential.

Take the time to reflect deeply on what each chapter offers you. Engage with the material not just intellectually, but emotionally and spiritually. This is your time to reconnect with who you truly are, to understand your deepest desires, and to take meaningful steps towards achieving the life you envision.

Enjoy the reading experience, savour each moment, and allow the lessons to unfold naturally. Let this book be more than just something you read—let it be a catalyst for profound change, growth, and the realisation of your fullest potential. Remember, this is your journey, and it's meant to be enjoyed every step of the way.

Part I

Introduction

THE JOURNEY BEGINS

Limlts Unleashed is not just a book; it's a mirror reflecting the struggles, doubts, and aspirations we all face. It tells the story of Kiritin, a boy born in a small town where the horizon seemed permanently out of reach. Growing up in a world that offered little hope, Kiritin's life was a labyrinth of uncertainty, with each twist and turn leading him deeper into a sense of loss and confusion—a feeling many of us know all too well.

From the start, Kiritin was burdened by self-doubt. He didn't know where to begin, whom to trust, or which path to follow. School was a battlefield, and every day he was told, in countless ways, that he was not enough. Labelled and dismissed as a boy who would never amount to much, a sentiment that stung deeply, Kiritin found solace in friendships. But even these were double-edged swords. His friends were the outcasts, the ones society had already written off: hawkers, street vendors, and petty wrongdoers.

In the eyes of his family, Kiritin was a failure waiting to happen. They feared he would become just another lost soul, a name whispered with pity or scorn. The welght of their disappointment was crushing, pushing him closer to a life that flirted with crime—a life where respect was earned through fear. The streets held an allure, a twisted promise of power and recognition, but deep down, Kiritin knew it was a path that led nowhere.

Sensing the peril, Kiritin's parents made a desperate choice. They sent him to the city—a world as different from his small town as night from day. The city was vast, blinding, and relentless. It magnified his insecurities, forcing him to confront the reality of how far behind he really was. Yet, by a stroke of fate, he found his way into college—a place where ambition was currency, and success was the only goal.

But college was no refuge. Kiritin was out of his depth, surrounded by sharp minds and sharper tongues. The ridicule cut deep, but it was nothing new. He had spent a lifetime being belittled, even by those who were supposed to believe in him. But this time, something within him snapped—not in anger, but in resolve. Tired of being the object of scorn, Kiritin took a hard look at his life. He asked himself the tough questions: Why was he here? What was holding him back? And most importantly, how could he change?

Kiritin looked up at the sky, searching for a guide who could help him navigate the tangled web of his life. In that moment of quiet desperation, he found his mentor—not in the world around him, but within himself—his inner voice, **Kisan**.

This moment of introspection was the spark that lit a fire in Kiritin's soul. He realised that the limits others had placed on him—and those he had accepted—were not walls, but illusions. They could be broken, but only if he had the courage to face them. With Kisan's guidance, Kiritin dug deep, pushing past long-held boundaries. He didn't just want to change his life; he wanted to rewrite it.

Today, Kiritin stands as a living testament to the power of transformation. His story is not one of overnight success, but of relentless perseverance. He refused to let his past define him and instead chose to define his future. His journey is a blueprint for anyone who has ever felt lost, doubted their potential, or dreamed of breaking free from the chains of mediocrity.

Kiritin's journey is unique, but the lessons are universal. In every challenge he faced, you can find your own struggles. In every victory he earned, you can find your own triumphs. This book is not just about overcoming obstacles—it's about unleashing the limitless potential within you. Like Kiritin, you can shape your destiny, overcome limits, and become your true self.

For young readers, Kiritin's journey under the mentorship of Kisan is a powerful lesson in discovering your own unique strengths—your superpowers. Just as Kiritin learned to navigate life by focusing on what he could do, rather than what he couldn't, you too will learn to recognise and nurture your strengths. This book will show you how to turn your abilities into tools for overcoming challenges and becoming the best version of yourself.

For young adults standing on the brink of their future, Kiritin's story offers inspiration and courage. *Limits Unleashed* encourages you to break free from societal pressures and internal doubts, just as Kiritin did, guided by Kisan's wisdom. His journey from a small town to success shows that dreaming beyond your circumstances has no limits.

And for those who have journeyed far, with wisdom earned through experience, Kiritin's later reflections—enriched by Kisan's insights—remind us that it's never too late to redefine our boundaries and explore new possibilities. His story is a beacon of hope, showing that even after years of struggle, growth and transformation are always within reach.

Ultimately, **Limits Unleashed** is about embracing the power that resides within you, just as Kiritin did with Kisan by his side. By understanding your limits—not as constraints, but as launchpads—you'll tap into a well of strength that leads to true growth and fulfilment. This book is your invitation to embark on a journey of self-discovery, to break through to new heights, and to unleash the limitless potential that lies within you. Like Kiritin, with Kisan's guidance, you have the power to transform your life—one limit at a time.

METROPOLIS AND THE MODERN

A Journey Through Kiritin's Eyes

Kiritin's journey parallels the fast-paced life of Metropolis, symbolising the universal struggle to navigate a world filled with constant demands and pressures. Just as Metropolis represents the relentless pursuit of success and the challenges that come with it, Kiritin's early life reflects confusion, a lack of direction, and the overwhelming nature of modern society. However, with the guidance of his inner-self mentor, Kisan, Kiritin learns to navigate this chaos and find his path.

From Chaos to Clarity: Kiritin's Metropolis

- Growing up in a small town, Kiritin felt lost and unsure, much like someone arriving in Metropolis for the first time. The city's hustle and bustle, with its towering skyscrapers and never-ending demands, mirror Kiritin's internal struggle to find his path in life. During this time of uncertainty, Kisan, his inner guide, begins to shape his journey.

- In his small town, Kiritin was overwhelmed by his environment, much like how Metropolis's citizens are engulfed by the constant need to achieve. Surrounded by negative influences and societal expectations, Kiritin's experience mirrors the culture of overdrive in Metropolis, where the pressure to succeed often leads to burnout and feelings of inadequacy. With Kisan's wisdom, Kiritin starts to see through the fog of these external pressures.

The Transition: A New Beginning in Metropolis

- When Kiritin moves to the big city, it symbolises his entry into Metropolis—a place where dreams are pursued with vigour but also where limits are tested. The blinding glare of the city represents Kiritin's initial overwhelm, mirroring how newcomers to Metropolis feel as they try to navigate the complexities of urban life. Kisan helps him ground himself amid this overwhelming change.

- Just as Metropolis's residents must find a balance between ambition and well-being, Kiritin's journey of self-discovery involves learning to manage his emotions, set boundaries, and find a path that aligns with his true self. Kisan's counsel becomes a crucial guide, reminding Kiritin of what truly matters amidst the city's chaos.

The Culture of Overdrive: Kiritin's Internal Struggles

- The culture of overdrive in Metropolis is reflected in Kiritin's desire to fit in and be seen as successful in the eyes of his peers and family. His struggles with studies and the pressure to conform to societal norms are akin to those of Metropolis's citizens, who push themselves beyond their limits in the pursuit of success. Here, Kisan's role is pivotal, helping Kiritin differentiate between true ambition and destructive pressure.

- Just as Metropolis teaches the importance of boundaries, Kiritin's story is about realizing his own limits and learning that true success comes from within—not from external validation. Kisan's presence is a constant reminder to Kiritin that success is not just about achieving but also about understanding and respecting his own boundaries.

Finding Balance: Kiritin's Transformation

- Kiritin's eventual success is a testament to the lessons of Metropolis and the wisdom of Kisan. He learns that while it's important to strive for greatness, it's equally crucial to know when to step back, reflect, and respect his own limits. His transformation from a directionless youth to a successful individual reflects how Metropolis's residents must learn to navigate the hustle without losing themselves, with Kisan's guidance as a compass.

- By embracing the LIMIT framework and with Kisan's mentorship, Kiritin, like the citizens of Metropolis, learns to harness his potential without succumbing to the pressures around him. His story is a reminder that in a world that never slows down, true success is found in balance, self-awareness, and the courage to know your limits.

🎯 Conclusion: Kiritin's Journey as a Microcosm of Metropolis

Kiritin's journey in *Limits Unleashed* is a microcosm of life in Metropolis—a city that embodies the modern hustle but also the need for boundaries and self-awareness. His story, enriched by Kisan's teachings, resonates with readers of all ages, showing that no matter where you start, the journey to success involves knowing your limits, embracing your strengths, and finding balance in a world that often pushes you to your breaking point. Through his journey and Kisan's wisdom, readers are reminded that true potential is unlocked not by endless striving, but by understanding and respecting their limits.

THE LIMIT FRAMEWORK

A Pathway to Personal and Professional Fulfilment

For billions of years, the universe has evolved through the relentless force of natural selection, shaping galaxies, ecosystems, and life itself. In much the same way, humans have adapted—not just physically, but by developing philosophies and tools that shape how we live, experience, and understand the world. Now, imagine for a moment: what if these guiding principles never existed? Without them, our lives would be directionless, lacking meaning and purpose.

Here's the truth: there is no one-size-fits-all solution to living a fulfilling life. That's why countless philosophies and tools have emerged, each offering its own lens through which we can navigate our journey. Today, you're about to encounter a powerful new framework—a system introduced by Kiritin's inner mentor, Kisan, that offers profound insight and clarity.

This unique framework, known as the "**LIMIT Framework**", guides individuals to focus on **Looking Inward, Interest, Mindset, Intent,** and **Trigger**. It's designed to help you navigate life's complexities while staying true to your values, aspirations, and authentic self. Kiritin's story is a vivid and inspiring testament to how the LIMIT Framework can transform lives, empowering us to thrive in a world that often feels overwhelming. Get ready to discover a philosophy that may just change how you see yourself and your place in the universe.

- **Looking Inward: Understanding and Respecting Boundaries**

Know Your Limit: In Kiritin's early life, the limits imposed by external factors—whether societal expectations, family pressures, or his own internalised beliefs—deeply influenced his sense of self. Growing up in a small town, he often felt not good enough, which made him afraid to fail and hesitant to step out of his comfort zone.

However, Kisan, serving as the voice of Kiritin's inner wisdom, guides him towards a crucial realization: the true essence of personal growth lies in Looking Inward. Kisan helps Kiritin understand that these external boundaries aren't definitive; they are merely perceptions that can be reshaped. By turning his focus inward, Kiritin learns that understanding his limits isn't about accepting constraints but about recognizing where his energy should be wisely invested.

This inward reflection allows Kiritin to identify his physical, emotional, and mental boundaries more clearly. He begins to appreciate the importance of setting realistic goals that align with his capabilities and prioritising self-care as a vital part of his journey. This inward shift in perspective empowers Kiritin to concentrate on what genuinely matters to him, steering clear of the pitfalls of overcommitment and the burnout that often accompanies it.

Through this process of Looking Inward, Kiritin starts to cultivate a sustainable approach to life—one that honours his intrinsic need for growth while safeguarding his well-being. He learns to focus on what he can control, gaining clarity, resilience, and a more fulfilling life.

- **Interest: Pursuing Your Passions**

Know Your Interest: As Kiritin transitions from his small town to the bustling life of the city, he is confronted with the stark reality of his own lack of direction. The city is filled with people who seem to have it all figured out—successful careers, clear goals, and a sense of purpose. Kiritin, on the other hand, feels lost and disconnected. This sense of alienation is a turning point, pushing him to explore what truly excites and motivates him.

Kisan guides Kiritin through the process of discovering his passions, encouraging him to reconnect with activities that bring him joy and fulfilment. This exploration of interest is a critical aspect of the LIMIT Framework. Kiritin learns that pursuing his passions is not just about finding a hobby or career path; it's about integrating these passions into his daily life in a way that keeps him energised and engaged. Through this process, Kiritin begins to understand that a life driven by genuine interest is not only more fulfilling but also more sustainable. This balance between passion and practicality becomes a cornerstone of his newfound sense of purpose.

- **Mindset: Cultivating a Growth-Oriented Perspective**

Know Your Mind: Kiritin's journey is marked by a profound shift in mindset, a transition from a fixed, fear-driven perspective to one of growth and resilience. Initially, Kiritin views the challenges he faces—whether in his academic pursuits, his social interactions, or his personal development—as insurmountable obstacles. He is plagued by self-doubt and a fear of failure, which prevent him from taking risks or pursuing his goals with confidence.

Kisan's mentorship plays a crucial role in transforming Kiritin's mindset. He introduces Kiritin to the concept of a growth mindset, where challenges are seen not as threats but as opportunities for learning and self-improvement. Kisan helps Kiritin understand that setbacks and failures are not reflections of his worth but rather stepping stones on the path to growth.

This new perspective empowers Kiritin to embrace challenges with a sense of curiosity and determination. Over time, he develops the resilience needed to navigate life's ups and downs, making continuous improvement a central theme in his journey.

- **Intent: Acting with Purpose**

Know Your Intent: The theme of intent in the LIMIT Framework is closely tied to Kiritin's search for meaning and direction in his life. For a long time, Kiritin's actions were driven by external expectations—what his family wanted, what society deemed successful, and what he thought he should be doing. This lack of alignment between his actions and his true desires left him feeling empty and unfulfilled.

Kisan challenges Kiritin to dig deeper, to ask himself the tough questions about why he does what he does. This introspection leads Kiritin to uncover his core values and the deeper motivations behind his goals. Kisan teaches him that intent is about more than just setting goals; it's about ensuring that those goals are aligned with his true self. This realization allows Kiritin to start making decisions that are not just practical but also meaningful. By acting with intent, Kiritin begins to live a life that is not only successful but also deeply satisfying. His actions become expressions of his true desires, leading to a more purposeful and fulfilling life.

- **Trigger: Managing Emotional Responses**

Know Your Trigger: Kiritin's emotional journey is one of the most compelling aspects of his story. Throughout his life, Kiritin is frequently overwhelmed by strong emotional responses, whether it's anxiety, frustration, or self-doubt. These emotions often stem from the societal and familial pressures he faces, as well as his own internal struggles with identity and self-worth. Left unchecked, these emotional triggers threaten to derail his progress, causing him to retreat into old, unproductive habits.

Kisan introduces Kiritin to the concept of emotional triggers and the importance of managing them effectively. This involves identifying the situations, people, or thoughts that provoke strong emotional reactions and developing strategies to cope with them. Kiritin learns techniques such as mindfulness, deep breathing, and cognitive reframing, which help him respond to triggers in a more balanced and thoughtful way. Over time, Kiritin becomes more adept at regulating his emotions, which is crucial for maintaining his mental and emotional well-being. This newfound emotional resilience allows him to stay focused on his goals and navigate life's challenges with greater ease.

🎯 Conclusion: Kiritin's Journey as a Reflection of the LIMIT Framework

Kiritin's story in *Limits Unleashed* is a powerful illustration of the LIMIT Framework in action. Each component of the framework— Looking Inward, Interest, Mindset, Intent, and Trigger—plays a vital role in his transformation from a directionless young man to a confident, purpose-driven individual. With Kisan's guidance, Kiritin learns to respect his limits, follow his passions, embrace growth, act with purpose, and manage emotions. This journey not only helps Kiritin achieve success in his personal and professional life but also brings him a deeper sense of fulfilment and happiness.

Kiritin's story serves as an inspiring example for readers, demonstrating how the principles of the LIMIT Framework can be applied to their own lives. By following Kiritin's journey and embracing the lessons of the LIMIT Framework, readers can learn to navigate the challenges of modern life with grace, resilience, and a sense of purpose.

(Looking Inward + Interest + Mindset + Intent + Trigger)

Get Ready for a Transformative Journey

Join Kiritin and his inner guide, Kisan, as they unlock the mysteries of the LIMIT Framework, breaking down every barrier Kiritin has ever known.

The next five chapters bring the LIMIT Framework to life, challenging you to reflect on your own journey. Are you chasing your dreams or playing it safe? Discover how to embrace change, recognise your turning points, and build a life where success, courage, and growth become your new normal.

The journey begins as Kiritin confronts self-doubt and uncovers his true potential. From there, dive into rediscovering his interests as Kisan guides Kiritin through self-reflection and old passions that reignite his purpose. As Kiritin masters the art of Mind Over Matter, the story deepens, showing him the path to mindfulness. Intent becomes the key to success, revealing that with the right focus, anything is possible.

But the most compelling part? It's about turning triggers into opportunities. Learn how Kiritin, with Kisan's help, transforms quick reactions into mindful responses. Kisan shares practical, real-world strategies that not only change Kiritin's life but can also impact yours.

Let's identify your core motivations ("Why"), set clear goals for your personal journey ("What"), and discover your own methods and strategies ("How") to unleash your true potential.

As you apply the LIMIT Framework to your daily life, you'll celebrate your courage and align with your true passions. Kiritin's journey may conclude, but yours is just beginning—a journey towards a life of limitless potential. This isn't just a story; it's a call to action.

Are you ready to unleash your limits?

Chapter 1

Mastering the Art of Control

A Deeper Dialogue Between Kiritin and Kisan

The morning sun rises over the bustling city of Metropolis, casting its golden rays on every corner, as if reminding the world that a new day has begun. Amid the chaos of the waking city, Kiritin finds a quiet bench, the noise of life around him fading into a distant hum. His thoughts are heavy, weighed down by uncertainty when suddenly Kisan, his inner voice, appears beside him—a silent yet powerful presence. Today, their conversation turns to a topic that will reshape Kiritin's journey: the circle of control.

Kiritin: (curious) Kisan, you mentioned that understanding what we can and cannot control is the key to a peaceful and fulfilling life. Can we explore these areas more deeply? What exactly falls within my circle of control, and what lies beyond it?

Kisan: (nodding) Of course, Kiritin. This understanding is the foundation of wisdom and contentment. Let's begin with what you can control. These are the elements directly influenced by your actions and mindset.

💡 <u>Things You Can Control</u>

- **Your Thoughts**

Kisan: Your mind is a powerful tool, Kiritin. The thoughts you choose to entertain shape your perception of reality. Negative thoughts can trap you in fear and doubt, while positive thoughts can lift you towards growth and achievement. While you may not control the initial thoughts that come to you, you can control whether you dwell on the. You can also replace them with something more empowering.

- **Your Actions**

Kisan: Every action you take is a choice, Kiritin. While you cannot control the outcome, you can control the effort you put in, the integrity with which you act, and the consistency you maintain. Your actions, day by day, create the path you walk.

- **Your Reactions**

Kisan: The world may throw challenges at you, but how you respond is entirely within your control. By mastering your reactions—whether through patience, calmness, or strategic thinking—you can turn obstacles into opportunities.

- **Your Attitude**

Kisan: Attitude is the lens through which you view the world. A positive attitude invites resilience and creativity, while a negative attitude closes doors. You have the power to choose an attitude of gratitude, optimism, or curiosity, regardless of your circumstances.

- **Your Effort**

Kisan: You can always control how much effort you put into something, whether it's your studies, work, relationships, or personal growth. Effort is one factor that is entirely up to you, and it often determines how far you can go.

- **Your Choices**

Kisan: Every moment presents choices, Kiritin. Some are significant, others small, but all are within your control. From the career path you follow to how you spend your free time, your choices define your journey.

- **How You Spend Your Time**

Kisan: Time is your most valuable resource. You control how you allocate it—whether you invest it in learning, building relationships, pursuing passions, or simply resting. How you use your time reflects your priorities and shapes your future.

- **Your Habits**

Kisan: Habits are the building blocks of your daily life. By cultivating good habits and breaking bad ones, you can steer your life in a direction that aligns with your goals and values.

Kiritin: (thoughtfully) I see how much power lies within these areas, Kisan. But what about the things I can't control? How do I deal with them without feeling helpless?

Kisan: (smiling) Ah, Kiritin, understanding what you cannot control is equally important. Recognising these areas allows you to let go of unnecessary burdens and focus your energy where it truly matters.

💡 <u>**Things You Can't Control**</u>

- **Your Birth**

Kisan: You did not choose where, when, or to whom you were born. Your birthplace, culture, and upbringing are not in your control. While they shape your early experiences, they do not determine your destiny. Your response to these circumstances is what counts.

- **Your Death**

Kisan: Life is finite, Kiritin. The exact moment and manner of your passing are beyond your control. Rather than fearing death, use this understanding to live each day with purpose, knowing that your time is limited.

- **Your Parents**

Kisan: You did not choose your parents, their values, or their expectations. While they influence you, you are not bound by their choices. Your path is yours to carve.

- **Your Past**

Kisan: The past is unchangeable. While it offers lessons, it should not hold you captive. What matters is how you use those lessons to shape your present and future.

- **Other People's Opinions**

Kisan: You cannot control what others think or say about you. Their opinions are a reflection of their own perspectives, not your worth. Seeking validation from others only distracts you from your true path.

- **Other People's Actions**

Kisan: Just as you control your actions, others control theirs. You cannot change how they behave, but you can choose how to respond. Focus on your own conduct and let go of the desire to control others.

- **Unexpected Events**

Kisan: Life is full of surprises—good and bad. Whether it's a natural disaster, an economic downturn, or a sudden opportunity, these events are beyond your control. What you can control is how you adapt and move forward.

- **The Outcome of Your Actions**

Kisan: You can give your best effort, but the results are not guaranteed. The outcome is influenced by countless factors beyond your control. Instead of fixating on results, focus on the process and the growth you experience along the way.

Kiritin: (realising) By letting go of what I cannot control, I can free myself from so much unnecessary stress. Instead of wasting energy on things I can't change, I can invest it in areas that truly matter.

Kisan: (encouragingly) Exactly, Kiritin. When you focus on what lies within your control, you empower yourself. You become resilient, adaptable, and at peace. And when you let go of what you cannot control, you find freedom—a freedom that allows you to live fully, with intention and joy.

Kiritin: (with a heavy sigh) Kisan, why do we always focus on what we don't have? Why is it so hard to appreciate what's already here, what we've already achieved? I feel like no matter how far I go, it's never enough.

Kisan: (thoughtfully) Ah, Kiritin, that feeling is one shared by many. We live in a world that constantly pushes us to want more—more success, more recognition, more possessions. But this endless chase creates an illusion of scarcity. We become so focused on what we lack that we forget the richness of what we already have.

Kisan pauses, his eyes scanning the park as if drawing wisdom from the surrounding nature.

Kisan: Gratitude is a powerful tool, Kiritin, but it takes practice. It's not about denying your ambitions or settling for less; it's about acknowledging the abundance already present in your life. Your mind is like a garden. If you water only the seeds of lack, they will grow into weeds of dissatisfaction. But if you tend to the seeds of gratitude, they will blossom into contentment and peace. You have more than you realise—you just need to shift your focus.

Kiritin: (nodding, but still uncertain) I hear you, but it feels like just being content isn't enough. What about greatness? How do I go from being good to great? Do I have to become famous or known by everyone to achieve something meaningful?

Kisan: (smiling) That's a common misconception. Greatness isn't tied to fame, Kiritin. Look at the people you admire. Many of them may be known, but what truly makes them great isn't their fame—it's their impact. It's the way they live, the values they embody, and the lives they touch. Everyone starts their journey from zero. Even the most revered figures in history had humble beginnings. The difference between good and great is not how many people know your name, but how you use your gifts, talents, and time to leave a mark.

Kisan's voice grows more introspective as he leans forward slightly, making his point clear.

Kisan: You see, a name is given to you by your parents, but it's your responsibility to make that name meaningful. It's not about seeking validation from the world. Greatness is born from consistency, integrity, and dedication to something greater than yourself. It's about working hard, even when no one is watching. True greatness is silent, often unnoticed at first. But over time, the impact is undeniable

> *"Your name is a gift from your parents, but it's your effort that turns it into a legacy."*

Kiritin: (thoughtfully) That makes sense, but why do I still feel trapped by self-doubt? It's like this constant voice in my head says, "What if you fail? What will people think of you?" It's exhausting, and sometimes it feels like it's holding me back from even trying.

Kisan: (gently) Doubt is natural, Kiritin. It's part of the human condition. But here's the thing—doubt isn't your enemy unless you let it be. Self-doubt arises when you start comparing yourself to others, when you forget your unique path. It comes when you place too much importance on what people think. Everyone fears failure at some point, but those who achieve greatness are the ones who push forward in spite of that fear.

Kisan places a hand on Kiritin's shoulder, his tone warm and encouraging.

Kisan: Remember, the people you spend time with influence your thoughts, your mindset, and your confidence. Look around at your circle—who do you surround yourself with? Are they lifting you up or feeding your doubts? Your environment matters, Kiritin. You can't always control who enters your life, but you can choose who you keep close. Surround yourself with those who inspire, challenge, and support you, and you'll find that your self-doubt starts to fade.

Kisan's gaze intensifies as he speaks his next words, as if imparting a lesson Kiritin must carry with him.

Kisan: About failure—what if you do fail? So what? Failure is not the end of your story. It's a stepping stone, a teacher. The world won't stop turning because you made a mistake. In fact, some of the greatest achievements in history were built on the backs of failure. What people say about you is beyond your control. Their opinions reflect their own insecurities, not your worth. Stop thinking, "Why did this happen to me?" and start asking, "What can I learn from this?" Heal yourself, Kiritin. Let go of the need for external validation and focus on your own growth.

> *"Experience stops you from making the same mistake twice, but the irony is you only get it by making mistakes in the first place."*

Kiritin listens intently, his expression shifting from one of uncertainty to one of realisation. He is beginning to understand the deeper meaning behind Kisan's words.

Kiritin: (softly) So, everything I need is already within me, isn't it?

Kisan: (with a nod) Yes, Kiritin. All the answers you seek are within you. You have the strength, the wisdom, and the ability to shape your life. The key is to trust yourself. When you stop worrying about what others think or what you lack, and when you let go of trying to control things beyond your reach, you'll realise that the only thing truly standing in your way is you.

Kisan pauses, allowing his words to sink in, before continuing with a softer tone.

Kisan: Life will throw challenges your way—that's inevitable. But it's how you respond to those challenges that will define your journey. Your ability to grow, to rise after falling, to learn from your missteps—that's what leads to greatness.

Kiritin's face softens as the weight of his doubts begins to lift. He feels lighter, as though he has just been given a map to navigate the labyrinth of his own mind.

Kiritin: (smiling slightly), I think I'm beginning to understand. It's not about fame or avoiding failure. It's about who I become in the process, the impact I make, and the people I keep around me.

Kisan: (with pride) Yes, exactly, Kiritin. And remember—every journey, no matter how great, begins with a single step. Don't be afraid to take it. Focus on what you can control: your thoughts, your actions, your attitude, and the effort you put into each day. The rest will unfold as it should.

They sit together in silence for a moment, the noise of the city around them growing fainter as Kiritin's mind grows clearer. He feels ready now, ready to step forward into the unknown, knowing that he carries the tools he needs within him.

Kiritin: (reflective) Kisan, there was a time when I struggled greatly with conversing in English. I felt out of place, embarrassed by my lack of fluency. I remember thinking, "If only I had been born and raised in a big city, I wouldn't be facing this problem." My rural upbringing felt like a chain holding me back. I thought the environment around me was the cause of my limitations.

Kisan: (gently) It's natural to feel that way, Kiritin. But consider this—what part of that situation was truly within your control?

Kiritin: (pausing) My birthplace, my early education... none of that was in my hands. But my effort to learn, my determination to improve—that was always mine to control. I didn't see it then, but I do now.

Kisan: (smiling) You've grasped the essence of the circle of control. The world isn't ideal, and we cannot change where we start. But we can change how we move forward. When you realised that your potential wasn't limited by your surroundings but by your mindset, everything began to shift. By embracing what you could control—your dedication and your practice—you transformed a perceived weakness into a strength.

Kiritin: (nodding, eyes shining with realization) Yes, and with that understanding, I focused on my communication skills. I practised relentlessly, not just to be average but to excel. Eventually, I worked with native speakers, refining my skills until I became proficient. I eventually started outperforming my own expectations.

Kisan: (proudly) That is the power of looking inward, Kiritin. By recognising your true potential and harnessing it, you shattered the limitations that once seemed insurmountable. Your journey is a testament to what can be achieved when we focus on what we can control and let go of what we cannot.

The conversation fades as Kiritin, filled with new resolve, looks towards the cityscape of Metropolis. The city once felt overwhelming, but now, with clarity and confidence, he knows that his path forward is clear. The shackles of doubt have been broken, replaced by a sense of purpose and an unshakable belief in his potential.

Action Step for Readers: Mastering the Art of Control

Harness the essence of the LIMIT Framework by focusing on the "L"—Looking Inward. The first step is mastering the art of control—focusing on what lies within your sphere of influence and letting go of what doesn't. Let's break this down into actionable steps that will help you gain greater control over your thoughts, actions, and mindset. This will also freeing you from unnecessary stress.

Reflection Exercise: Identifying What You Can and Cannot Control

- Step 1: Take out a notebook or journal. Draw two columns on a blank page.
- Step 2: Label the first column as "Things I Can Control" and the second as "Things I Can't Control."
- Step 3: Under the "Can Control" column, write down everything that you have direct influence over— your thoughts, actions, attitude, effort, habits, time management, and choices. Be as specific as possible.
- Step 4: In the "Can't Control" column, list things like other people's opinions, unexpected events, your past, your birth circumstances, or outcomes that are outside your control. Again, be as detailed as possible.
- Step 5: Reflect on how much time you spend worrying about the items in the "Can't Control" column. This awareness is the first step towards freeing yourself from unnecessary burdens.

Daily Mindfulness: Focus on What You Can Control

- Affirmation: Every morning, take a moment to remind yourself of what you can control today. Say it out loud or write it down as an affirmation:

  "I focus on what I can control: my thoughts, my actions, and my effort.". Throughout the day, whenever stress or anxiety creeps in, return to this affirmation. Consciously shift your energy toward things within your control, letting go of concerns about external factors.

Mindset Shift: Reframe Your Inner Dialogue

- Challenge Negative Thoughts: When self-doubt or fear of failure arises, notice these thoughts and ask yourself, "Is this something I can control?" If the answer is no, release it. Replace the negative thought with a positive or actionable one.

  For example, instead of worrying, "What if I fail?", ask, "What can I learn from this experience regardless of the outcome?"

- Self-Compassion: When you face setbacks, don't fall into the trap of thinking, "Why did this happen to me?" Instead, practice self-compassion by saying, "This is a learning opportunity. I will grow from this."

Strengthening Your Circle: Audit Your Environment

- Evaluate Relationships: Take a closer look at the people you spend time with. Are they helping you grow, or do they contribute to your doubts and fears? Make it a priority to surround yourself with people who encourage you to be your best self.
- Action Step: Reach out to a mentor, friend, or colleague who inspires you. Spend more time with people who challenge you to think positively and act with integrity.
- Cultivate Positive Influences: Be mindful of the content you consume—social media, news, and entertainment. Choose sources that uplift and motivate you, rather than those that feed negativity or self-doubt.

Commitment to Growth: Developing New Habits

- Build Good Habits: Identify a habit you'd like to develop that aligns with your goals. Start small and commit to practising it daily. Whether it's reading for personal development, exercising, or meditating, consistency is key.

- Break Bad Habits: Identify a habit that isn't serving you—such as procrastination or negative self-talk. Replace it with a positive action. For example, instead of scrolling aimlessly through social media, set a timer for focused work or learning.

Purposeful Use of Time: Prioritise What Matters

- Action Plan: At the start of each week, set aside time to plan your priorities. Identify the most important tasks that align with your goals and values. Allocate time for them first, ensuring that your time reflects your intentions.

- Time Journal: Keep track of how you spend your time for a week. At the end of the week, reflect on whether your time aligned with your goals. Make adjustments to ensure that you're investing your time wisely.

Letting Go: Release What You Can't Control

- Mental Exercise: At the end of each day, review your "Can't Control" column. Take a deep breath and mentally release any worries related to these items. Remind yourself that worrying won't change these things. Your energy is also better spent on what you can influence.

- Visualization: Close your eyes and imagine physically placing the items from your "Can't Control" list into a box. Then, mentally "set the box aside" as a symbol of letting go.

Celebrate Your Progress: Acknowledge Your Efforts

- Celebrate Small Wins: Each week, reflect on one area where you have successfully focused on what you could control. Celebrate this win, no matter how small it may seem.
- Write it down: "This week, I took control of ______. I am proud of my effort and growth."
- Daily, remind yourself that life is a continuous journey of growth, learning, and transformation. By mastering what you can control and letting go of the rest, you not only reduce stress but also unlock your potential to live more fully and authentically. Remember, greatness isn't about perfection – it's about progress.

Readers' Notes:

❍ **Mantra for Daily Practice** ❍

Identify what's beyond your control and redirect your energy towards what you can—transform your focus, transform your life.

Chapter 2

Rediscovering Interest

A tranquil forest, where the sunlight filters through the thick canopy, casting a serene glow on the moss-covered ground. The air is thick with the scent of earth and leaves. Kiritin, weighed down by doubt and confusion, sits beneath a towering, ancient tree. His brow furrows as he contemplates his life's direction, feeling lost and adrift. From the silence, Kisan, his inner self mentor, appears beside him—serene, wise, and glowing with an ethereal light.

Kiritin: (voice trembling, eyes downcast) Kisan, I feel like I'm standing at a crossroads, but the path ahead is shrouded in darkness. My life seems void of meaning, and the purpose I once felt has slipped away like sand through my fingers. Where do I go from here? What should I do?

Kisan: (smiling gently, his presence calming) Kiritin, it's natural to face such dilemmas on the journey of life. Just as the sun's light can be hidden by thick clouds, so too can your purpose be obscured by doubt and uncertainty. But remember, within you lies the power to disperse these clouds. Let us explore this together.

Kisan pauses, allowing his words to sink in. His gaze is soft and encouraging, a beacon in Kiritin's fog of confusion.

"Tell me, Kiritin, what is one thing you could do for hours without feeling bored or tired?"

Kiritin: (after a moment of introspection) I find peace in teaching others. When I share knowledge, time seems to stand still. I could teach for hours and still feel invigorated, not drained.

Kisan: (nodding with understanding) This, Kiritin, is your passion. It is one of the pillars of your Ikigai, your reason for being. Yet, passion alone cannot guide you to your true purpose. Consider this: Does the career path you've chosen allow you to nurture this love for teaching? Does it align with what truly excites and fulfils you?

Kiritin: (with a sigh, eyes reflecting inner turmoil) I chose my career out of necessity, not passion. It provides for me, yes, but my spirit feels empty. I've often wondered if I'm on the wrong path. Kiritin's voice quivers as he speaks, revealing the depth of his discontent. His job, though stable and secure, has become a source of growing dissatisfaction. Each day feels like a step further away from the life he truly desires. His heart longs for the joy he finds in teaching, but his mind is shackled by the fear of stepping into the unknown.

Kisan: (with empathy) This is the influence of dilemma, Kiritin. The world often tells us to choose paths of security and stability, but true fulfilment comes when we align our work with what we love and what we are naturally good at. Tell me, do you believe you are good at teaching? Does it benefit others?

Kiritin: (thoughtfully) Yes, I believe so. My students often express gratitude, and it brings me great joy to see them grow and understand. Their success feels like my own.

Kisan: (his voice filled with wisdom) Then you have discovered another element of your Ikigai[1]—your vocation. You are not only passionate about teaching but skilled at it, and it benefits others. However, your purpose extends beyond these. It also encompasses how you can serve the world and sustain yourself. Have you considered how your passion for teaching could fulfil a greater societal need and support your livelihood?

Kiritin's mind races as he reflects on Kisan's words. He recalls the times he felt torn between his passion for teaching and the financial stability of his current job. This internal conflict had created a chasm between his dreams and his reality, leading to a growing discontent that had begun to erode his sense of purpose.

Kiritin: (puzzled, yet curious) I've never thought of it that way, Kisan. I always saw teaching as a passion, something separate from a profession that could sustain me.

Kisan: (with gentle guidance) This is where the concept of Ikigai becomes powerful, Kiritin. Your purpose lies at the intersection of what you love, what you are good at, what the world needs, and what you can be paid for. To find your true

---

1   *Ikigai: The Japanese Secret to a Long and Happy Life*—a reason for living. Having a strong sense of *ikigai*—where what you love, what you're good at, what you can get paid for, and what the world needs all overlap—means that each day is infused with meaning.

path, you must seek to integrate these elements. Imagine a life where your work is not just a job but a calling that fulfils all these aspects.

Kiritin's eyes widen as he begins to see the bigger picture. He realises that he has been living in fragments, with his passion, profession, and purpose existing in silos. The thought of merging these elements excites him; it rekindles a flame that had long been extinguished by routine and conformity.

Kiritin: (with dawning realisation) You're right, Kisan. I've been looking at my life in fragments, not as a whole. My interests, my skills, my contributions to the world—all these must align for me to find true fulfilment.

Kisan: (encouraging) Exactly, Kiritin. This is why knowing your purpose is so vital. When your interests guide your actions, they bring clarity, motivation, and joy. They transform mundane tasks into meaningful endeavours. But remember, your purpose is not just about following hobbies—it's about discovering the deeper passions that resonate within you, the ones that can drive your career and your contribution to the world.

Kiritin feels a wave of clarity wash over him. He recognises that his discontent stemmed from ignoring his inner voice, from suppressing the passions that had once defined him. Now, with Kisan's guidance, he is ready to reclaim those lost parts of himself.

> *"Knowing your interest is knowing your true self. A fish thrives in water, not on branches. Embrace your true path, and it will lead you to fulfilment."*

Kiritin: (resolutely) I see now, Kisan. I must look deeper, beyond the surface of my daily life. I must find what truly excites and energises me, what I am naturally skilled at, and how I can use these gifts to serve others and build a fulfilling life.

Kisan: (smiling gently) Yes, Kiritin. This is your path to rediscovering your interest. Ask yourself these questions: What do I love? What am I good at? What does the world need that I can offer? And how can I make a living doing this? By reflecting on these questions, you will uncover your Ikigai, your true reason for being.

Kiritin's heart feels lighter as he contemplates these questions. The doubts that had once clouded his mind begin to dissipate, replaced by a renewed sense of purpose and direction. He understands now that his journey is not about choosing between security and passion, but about finding the harmony between them.

Kiritin: (grateful, his heart lightened) Thank you, Kisan. You have illuminated the path before me. I will take these questions to heart and begin my journey of rediscovery. I now understand that my potential is limitless when I align my interests with my purpose.

Kisan: (with wisdom) Go forth, Kiritin. But before you go, let me share an example that might resonate with you. Think of a young woman I once guided, who faced a similar crossroads. She had a secure job in finance, something she was good at but didn't love. Her true passion lay in social entrepreneurship, in creating opportunities for the underprivileged. The world needed what she had to offer, but fear of uncertainty held her back. With time, she realised that her purpose was to combine her financial acumen with her desire to make a difference. She left her job, took the risk, and started a social enterprise. Today, she's not only fulfilled, but she's also making a tangible impact on the lives of others, and yes, she's sustaining herself well. Her passion, skills, societal contribution, and livelihood all aligned. That is Ikigai, Kiritin.

Kiritin listens intently, the story striking a deep chord within him. He thinks of his own passion for teaching and the desire to make a difference in the lives of underprivileged youth in his hometown.

Kiritin: (inspired) I've been facing a similar decision, Kisan. I've always wanted to empower the youth in my hometown, to give them opportunities I never had. But I've been afraid—afraid of failing, afraid of what society would say if I left my stable job. Yet, hearing this story, I realise that I have the skills, the passion, and the drive to make it work. I can teach, mentor, and inspire them, just as you've guided me.

Kisan: (with wisdom) Go forth, Kiritin. Remember that the journey of life is about embracing your inner self, understanding your true passions, and letting them guide you to a life of purpose, fulfilment, and joy. The LIMIT framework is your guide, and in it, 'I' stands for Interest—the very core of your being. Trust in your abilities and let your passion guide you. The world needs what you have to offer.

Kiritin rises from his seat beneath the ancient tree, filled with a renewed sense of purpose. The clouds of doubt have lifted, and the path ahead, though challenging, is now illuminated by the light of self-discovery and purpose. He bows to Kisan, who smiles knowingly, understanding that Kiritin is now ready to embark on his true journey.

This conversation not only touches upon Kiritin's struggle with direction but also deeply explores how discovering one's purpose, through the framework of Ikigai, can lead to a more fulfilling and meaningful life. The dialogue integrates themes of **dilemma**, **growing discontent**, **self-reflection**, and **rekindling old passions**—all while guiding the reader to apply these insights to their own lives using the LIMIT framework.

🤝 <u>Action Step for Readers: Rediscovering Interest</u>

To effectively rediscover your interests and align them with your life's purpose, the LIMIT framework offers a structured approach that enhances the clarity and depth of your self-exploration. The 'I' in LIMIT stands for Interest, emphasising the importance of connecting with what genuinely excites and fulfils you By reflecting on what you love, what you're good at, how it helps others, and how it can earn you a living. Combining these answers can guide you toward a fulfilling life.

The LIMIT framework doesn't just guide you to uncover your interests; it provides a holistic approach to integrating those interests into a life of purpose. It helps you move beyond superficial passions to discover the deeper drives that can fuel a career aligned with your values and strengths. This alignment brings multiple benefits: increased motivation, greater clarity in decision-making, and a profound sense of satisfaction that comes from knowing you're living in accordance with your true self.

The following step-by-step process will help you move beyond fleeting passions and connect with your deeper drives – those that can fuel both your personal and professional life.

Reflect on What You Love (Passion Discovery)

- **Exercise:** Take a moment today to reflect on the activities, hobbies, or tasks that make you feel energised and alive. What do you do that makes time seem to fly by? These are clues to your passions.
- **Affirmation:** "I am in tune with the activities that bring me joy and energy, and I honour these as clues to my passions."
- **Action:** Write down at least five things you genuinely enjoy doing. These could range from creative pursuits like painting or writing to problem-solving, teaching, or organising events. Allow yourself to dream without limitations or expectations—this is your time to explore what truly excites you.

Identify Your Strengths (Skills and Talents)

- **Exercise:** Consider your top strengths and skills—those things you naturally excel at or have developed over time.

Reflect on the activities where you consistently perform well and receive positive feedback.

- **Affirmation:** "I recognise and appreciate my unique strengths and talents, and I am proud of how they align with my passions."
- **Action:** Make a list of these strengths. Ask yourself, "What am I really good at?" and "How do these strengths align with the things I love?" You might also seek feedback from others, as they can often identify talents that you might overlook in yourself. Write down these insights and note how they relate to the passions you identified earlier.

Analyse the Impact (How You Benefit Others)

- **Exercise:** Reflect on how your passions and skills can positively impact others. Think about the ways in which you can contribute to the well-being, growth, or happiness of others through your unique abilities.
- **Affirmation:** "I understand the positive impact I can have on others through my passions and strengths, and I am committed to making a difference."
- **Action:** Consider how you have already made a difference in others' lives, whether it's through teaching, helping, creating, or inspiring. Write down who benefits from your strengths and how you can continue or expand this impact. For example, if you love writing and are skilled at storytelling, perhaps your words can inspire or educate others.

Consider Livelihood (Turn Passion into a Profession)

- **Exercise:** Think about how you can turn your passions into something that supports you financially. Explore potential career paths, business opportunities, or side projects that align with your passions, skills, and the impact you want to make.

- **Affirmation:** "I am capable of turning my passions into a profession that brings me both fulfilment and financial support."
- **Action:** Ask yourself, "How can I turn my interests into a sustainable livelihood?" Research careers, freelance opportunities, or entrepreneurial ventures where your skills and passions can thrive. Write down potential ideas, no matter how big or small. Consider how they could evolve into something that integrates your passion into your profession.

Set Clear Goals (Action Plan to Move Forward)

- **Exercise:** Create a detailed action plan to start incorporating these insights into your life. Start small with achievable goals and gradually build on them to create momentum towards larger aspirations.
- **Affirmation:** "I set clear, achievable goals that align my life with my passions, strengths, and the impact I wish to make."
- **Action:** Break down your plan into actionable steps. For example, if your goal is to transition into a career that aligns with your passion for teaching, start by taking a relevant course, volunteering to teach, or networking with professionals in the field. Set short-term goals (e.g., "Within one month, I will complete a course on online teaching") and long-term goals (e.g., "Within a year, I will launch my own online teaching platform"). Regularly review and adjust your goals as you progress.

By following the LIMIT framework, you will not only rediscover your interests but also transform them into meaningful actions that resonate with who you are at your core. This journey leads to a more fulfilling and balanced life, where your work and passions are not separate entities but harmoniously intertwined.

Readers' Notes:

 **Mantra for Daily Practice**

Identify the very core of your being and
let your true nature guide what you have to
offer to the world.

Chapter 3

Mind Over Matter

Kiritin's brow furrows as he contemplates the direction of his life. Each path he envisions feels like a dead end, leading him further from the sense of purpose he once knew. The life he has built, the goals he has pursued—everything suddenly seems devoid of meaning. He tries to focus on the present, on the beauty around him, but his mind is a turbulent sea of doubts, with crashing waves of insecurity and fear battering his resolve. As he closes his eyes, seeking clarity, Kisan, his inner mentor, appears beside him, radiating calm and wisdom.

Kiritin:(in a weary voice) Kisan, my mind is in turmoil. Work stress, emotional triggers, and the constant pressure of balancing my life have left me feeling overwhelmed. How do I find peace? How do I master my mind amidst this chaos?

Kisan: (with a gentle smile) Kiritin, the mind is a powerful tool, but it can also be our greatest adversary if left unchecked. The Bhagavad Gita[2] speaks of the mind as both a friend and a foe.

---

2 *Bhagavad Gita: The Bhagavad Gita, often referred to as the Gita, is a Hindu scripture, dated to the second or first century BCE, which forms part of the Epic Mahabharata. It is a synthesis of various strands of Indian thought and religion, including the Vedic concept of dharma; Samkhya-based yoga and Jnana; and Bhakti.*

When controlled, it serves us well; when uncontrolled, it leads to suffering. Let us explore how you can know and control your mind, for it is the key to mastering your life.

Knowing and Controlling Your Mind

Kisan: The first step, Kiritin, is to understand the nature of your mind. The mind is like a restless monkey, constantly jumping from one thought to another, often dwelling on worries and fears. This "monkey mind" can create unnecessary stress and anxiety, clouding your judgment and disturbing your peace. Controlling your mind is essential for several reasons:

- **Awareness:** Begin by noticing your thoughts without judgment. Become an observer of your mind, watching the flow of thoughts as if they were clouds passing through the sky. This practice of mindfulness allows you to see your mental habits—whether they are fantasies, worries, or recurring negative thoughts—without becoming entangled in them.

- **Self-Talk:** Your internal dialogue, or self-talk, is a powerful force that shapes your emotions and actions. If your self-talk is negative, it will drag you down; if it is positive, it will lift you up. By consciously changing your self-talk, you can influence your mindset and emotional well-being.

- **Focus on Positivity:** The mind has a natural tendency to focus on negative experiences, a phenomenon known as the "negativity bias." This can lead to a cycle of pessimism and stress. Counteract this by deliberately focusing on positive experiences and savouring them. This practice will help you rewire your brain to be more resilient and optimistic.

- **Label Your Emotions:** When you feel overwhelmed by emotions, simply naming them—saying "I am feeling anxious" or "I am feeling stressed"—can help calm your mind. This activates the logical part of your brain, reducing the intensity of the emotion and allowing you to regain control.

Kisan: To master your mind, Kiritin, you must take deliberate action. Here is a step-by-step plan to help you gain control:

- **Notice Your Mental Habits:** Begin by paying attention to your thoughts. Notice when your mind wanders, when it fixates on worries, or when it spirals into negativity. This awareness is the first step toward change.

- **Change Your Self-Talk:** Identify any negative or self-critical thoughts and consciously replace them with positive affirmations. For example, instead of saying, "I can't handle this," tell yourself, "I am capable and strong." Practice this regularly, and you will notice a shift in your mindset.

- **Focus on Positive Experiences:** Each day, take time to reflect on positive moments. When something good happens, pause to savour it for at least five seconds. This simple practice will help strengthen your brain's positivity pathways.

- **Label Your Thoughts:** When your mind starts to spin stories or worries, label them with simple phrases like "just thoughts" or "thinking." This practice, derived from mindfulness meditation, helps you distance yourself from the mental chatter. You will also see your thoughts more objectively.

- **First Steps Toward Mindfulness:** Start with small mindfulness practices—taking deep breaths, focusing on the present moment, or practising gratitude. These steps will help you cultivate a more peaceful and focused mind.

Kiritin:(confused, pacing back and forth) Thank you, Kisan. However, why does it all feel so pointless? I'm stuck. I keep pushing myself, but it feels like I'm getting nowhere. I want to succeed, but I'm starting to lose hope. Everyone else seems to have it figured out, and here I am, stuck in the same place.

Kisan: (calmly, his voice like a soft breeze) Kiritin, do you remember what I once told you? Everything begins with a thought. Every action, every decision, every moment of success—it all starts with a single spark in your mind. If your thoughts are clouded with doubt, how can you expect the world outside to be clear?

Kiritin:(pauses, running his hands through his hair) So it's all in my head? But thoughts alone won't bring me success. Everywhere I look, people talk about shortcuts. Why can't I just find one? Why does it have to be so hard?

Kisan: (firmly, yet empathetically) There are no shortcuts to success, Kiritin. Imagine a farmer planting seeds in his field. He can't expect to see a harvest tomorrow, can he? No. He waits, nurtures, and gives it time. Success is like that—it grows slowly, steadily, like a tree whose roots deepen with time. You may see others with quick successes, but those are often like houses built on sand. When the storm comes, they crumble. Real success is built brick by brick, with patience and persistence.

Kiritin: (sighing, staring at the ground) But how do I even know if what I'm doing is the right thing? What if I'm wasting my time on something that only gives me short-term gains, and in the end, I'm left with nothing?

Kisan: That's where you need clarity, Kiritin. The difference between long-term and short-term success is like the difference between building a temporary shelter and constructing a home. Sure, you could build a small hut to shield you from a night's storm, but what about the future? Wouldn't you rather put in the effort to build a house, one that will stand strong for years? Long-term success is about seeing beyond the immediate, about investing in something that lasts. Short-term gains may give you temporary satisfaction, but long-term success provides true fulfilment.

Kiritin:(his voice softer, unsure) I understand that, but sometimes, I feel like I'm putting in so much effort and seeing so little in return. It's exhausting. Why does it feel like I'm chasing something I'll never catch?

Kisan: (smiling gently) That's because you're doing things with the expectation of immediate rewards. You need to learn the art of doing things without expecting anything in return. True mastery comes when you can put your heart into your work simply because it brings you joy or fulfilment. It won't happen if you're waiting for applause or recognition. Take, for example, a musician who plays not for the crowd but for the love of the music itself. When you pour your energy into something without expecting, you free yourself from disappointment.

Kiritin: (thoughtfully, looking up at Kisan) But is it wrong to expect something when you work hard for it? Isn't that natural?

Kisan: It's human, yes. But expectations can trap you. When you work only for the result, you tie your happiness to an outcome that's often out of your control. Think of the sun. It rises every morning, giving warmth and life to all, without asking for anything in return. Does it expect the world to be grateful for its light? No. It simply shines because that's its nature. Live like that, Kiritin—give your best without constantly weighing the outcome. Let the joy of your work be enough.

Kiritin:(letting out a heavy sigh) It's just… life seems to be all about balance. It's hard to know where to draw the line between working hard and knowing when to let go, between ambition and peace. How do I balance everything?

Kisan: (nodding thoughtfully) Ah, balance. Life is indeed a dance of balance. It's never as simple as success or failure, black or white. There's always a middle ground, a grey area where real life happens. Think of a tightrope walker. Their success isn't in rushing to the end of the rope but in maintaining balance as they move forward. The same goes for life—it's not about always winning or never failing, but about finding the balance in between. You must learn to navigate that middle ground. It's where you'll find peace, even in the midst of chaos.

Kiritin: (frowning) I understand that, but I can't help comparing myself to others. Every time I see someone doing better than me, it eats me up inside. It makes me feel like I'm failing.

Kisan: (smiling softly) Kiritin, you're running a race that has only one competitor—yourself. Comparing yourself to others is a losing battle. The best competition you can engage in is with the person you were yesterday. Why should someone else's success define your own? Compete with yourself. Strive to be better today than you were yesterday. That's where true growth comes from. And as for motivation, why seek it from others? You hold the power to motivate yourself. Your goals, your dreams—let them fuel your drive. You don't need the world's approval to chase your dreams.

Kiritin: (nodding slowly) But what if I'm lying to myself? What if I think I'm working hard, but deep down, I know I'm not giving it my all? How do I face that truth?

Kisan:(his voice serious) You can cheat the world, Kiritin, but you can never cheat yourself. Deep down, you know the truth. Your conscience will always remind you if you're falling short, even if you try to ignore it. Be honest with yourself. That's the foundation of real progress. If you're not giving your best, only you can change that. Don't look for excuses; face your truth head-on.

Kiritin: (with a slight grin) So, I should treat myself like a celebrity then? Like someone worth investing in?

> *"You can fool everyone else, but not yourself. Real progress starts when you stop ignoring your conscience and face the truth."*

Kisan: (laughs warmly) Not in vanity, but in empowerment. Treat yourself like someone who is capable of great things. Believe in your potential. When you treat yourself with respect and believe in your abilities, you unlock a power within you. Self-empowerment is not about thinking you're above others; it's about recognizing your own worth and striving to live up to it.

Kiritin: (thoughtfully) I've heard something about focusing on the 80-20 rule. What does that really mean?

Kisan: The 80/20 principle is simple. It teaches you that 20% of your efforts produce 80% of your results. The key is focusing on the things that truly matter—the vital few. Instead of spreading your energy across everything, find those critical tasks or actions that will have the most impact and give them your full attention. Prioritise wisely, and you'll see greater returns for your efforts.

Kiritin: (nodding but still uncertain) But sometimes, even with all my effort, things don't work out. It's like luck plays a bigger role than hard work.

Kisan: Luck does play a part, but remember, Kiritin, life is a combination of destiny and design. Some things are beyond your control, but others are shaped by your actions. Sometimes, you'll work hard and not see the results you want. Other times, without any expectation, something good will come your way. Life is a game of probability. But whether you succeed or fail, what matters most is what you learn from each experience.

Kiritin: (softly) I guess I need to celebrate my failures too, then?

Kisan: Absolutely. Failure is not the end—it's part of the journey. Every time you stumble, you learn something new. Celebrate your failures because they are stepping stones to your success.

Without them, you wouldn't grow, adapt, or evolve. Each failure makes you stronger and wiser.

Kiritin: (smiling, more assured) So, every day, I should focus on becoming a better version of myself?

Kisan: Precisely. Success doesn't come overnight. It's the result of consistent effort, day after day. Even athletes, who shine in a five-minute performance, train for years in the shadows. It's their daily commitment, their consistency, that leads them to those moments of glory.

Kiritin: But as I get older, I find it harder to take risks. It's like I'm slowing down, but I see others moving ahead.

Kisan: That's natural, Kiritin. As we grow older, the weight of responsibilities makes us cautious. But those who maintain their pace, who remain consistent in their efforts, continue to move ahead. If you slow down out of fear, you risk falling behind. Consistency is key. Life is like the seasons—it changes constantly. You need to adapt to those changes and keep moving forward.

Kiritin: (thoughtfully) And what if I face problems along the way?

Kisan: Be a problem solver, not just someone who raises issues and waits for others to resolve them. Life will always throw challenges your way. But don't just sit there—find solutions. And sometimes, to solve problems, you must unlearn what you know. What worked yesterday might not work today. Be flexible, be open to change.

Kiritin: (smiling, his mind clearer) I understand now. It's not about rushing to the end, but about finding balance, growing steadily, and being open to learning, even through failure.

Kisan: (with a proud smile) Exactly, Kiritin. Life is an art of balance, patience, and resilience. Keep moving forward, without fear of the outcome. You will always be better for the journey, no matter where it leads.

Kiritin: (with renewed determination) I see now that my mind is not my enemy but a tool that I can master. I will take these steps to heart and begin my journey towards mindfulness and mental mastery.

Kisan: (with a serene smile) Remember, Kiritin, mastering the mind is not a one-time effort but a lifelong practice. True wisdom comes from understanding the self and controlling the mind. As you embark on this journey, let your mind become your ally, guiding you towards peace, purpose, and fulfilment.

Kiritin: (with a pensive look) Kisan, I've been thinking a lot about what you've said. I remember a time when I was terrified of public speaking. Whenever I had to give a talk, I'd feel a surge of anxiety. My hands would shake, and my mind would go completely blank.

Kisan: (nodding thoughtfully) Public speaking is a common challenge for many people. It's understandable to feel overwhelmed. What did you find most difficult about it?

Kiritin: (sighing) It felt like every time I stood in front of an audience, I was facing a wall of judgment. I'd worry about making mistakes, forgetting my points, or not being able to engage with the audience. I kept thinking that if I had known how to control my mind better, I might have been able to handle it more effectively.

Kisan: (encouragingly) It's good that you recognise that. Controlling your mind is indeed key to overcoming such challenges. How did you approach overcoming this fear?

Kiritin:(reflecting) I started by acknowledging my feelings of anxiety instead of trying to ignore them. I began practising relaxation techniques like deep breathing and visualisation to calm myself before speaking. I also focused on positive experiences and used affirmations to counter my negative thoughts. Over time, with consistent practice, I noticed a significant improvement.

Kisan: (smiling) That's a great start. Acknowledging your feelings helps you understand and address them rather than letting them control you. Developing relaxation techniques like deep breathing helps manage physical symptoms of anxiety. Focusing on positive experiences and using positive self-talk can shift your mindset from fear to confidence.

Kiritin: (with a nod) Yes, and I found that regular practice was crucial. The more I practised speaking, the more comfortable I became. It's like training a muscle – the more you work on it, the stronger it gets.

Kisan: Precisely. With hard work, dedication, and determination, you can unlock your true potential and achieve your goals. The mind, when properly trained and controlled, can transform challenges into opportunities.

Kiritin: (with renewed determination) I understand now. By preparing my mind and practicing regularly, I can overcome my fears and perform better. I see how important it is to keep working on these strategies.

Kisan: (with encouragement) Exactly, Kiritin. Mastering your mind is a continuous journey. As you keep practising and applying these techniques, you'll find that what once seemed daunting becomes manageable, and you'll be able to achieve more than you thought possible.

Kiritin: (smiling) Thank you, Kisan. Your guidance has given me a clearer path forward. I feel more confident about tackling my fears and achieving my goals.

Kisan: (with a serene smile) Remember, Kiritin, the journey to mastering the mind is ongoing. Stay committed to your practice, and let your mind be your ally in achieving peace and fulfilment.

Kiritin: (rising with resolve) I will. Thank you for helping me see how to transform my fear into strength.

Kisan: (nodding approvingly) You're welcome, Kiritin. Embrace the challenge with confidence, and you'll continue to grow and succeed.

Kiritin rises, his mind clearer and more focused. He bows to Kisan, who smiles knowingly, understanding that Kiritin is ready to embrace the challenge of mastering his mind and finding balance in his life.

 <u>Action Step for Readers: Mastering Your Mind</u>

As you reflect on the conversation between Kiritin and Kisan, here are practical steps you can take to start mastering your mind: Begin by observing your mental habits without judgment, recognising whether your thoughts lean towards negativity, anxiety, or criticism. Next, consciously shift your self-talk to be more positive and affirming, reinforcing this new mindset daily. Focus on positive experiences, taking time each day to savour and reflect on them, which helps rewire your brain towards optimism. Label your thoughts to create distance from them, reducing their emotional impact. Incorporate mindfulness practices, even starting with just five minutes a day, to train your mind to stay present. Lastly, apply the "Know Your LIMIT" framework, particularly emphasising the importance of a positive mindset, as it's the foundation of your mental well-being and resilience. Here are practical, affirmative exercises to help you begin mastering your mind. These will also help you foster a sense of balance and growth in your life:

Observe Without Judgment

- Exercise: Start each day by taking 5-10 minutes to observe your thoughts. Sit quietly, close your eyes, and notice the thoughts passing through your mind without reacting to them. Are they positive, negative, anxious, or self-critical? Just observe.
- Affirmation: "I am aware of my thoughts, but I am not controlled by them. I observe my mind with clarity and peace."

Shift to Positive Self-Talk

- Exercise: Throughout the day, catch yourself when your self-talk turns negative or critical. For every negative thought, replace it with a positive affirmation. For example, if you catch yourself thinking, "I can't do this," immediately replace it with, "I am capable of overcoming challenges."
- Affirmation: "I choose empowering, uplifting thoughts. My words shape my reality."

Focus on Positive Experiences

- Exercise: At the end of each day, write down three positive things that happened. These can be small moments, like enjoying a cup of coffee, receiving a kind word, or accomplishing a task. Reflect on these moments and take time to fully savour them.
- Affirmation: "I acknowledge and celebrate the positive experiences in my life, no matter how small."

Label Your Thoughts for Clarity

- Exercise: When you notice your mind spiralling into anxiety or worry, pause and label the thoughts. For example, say to yourself, "This is just worry," or "This is fear." By labelling the thought, you create distance from it and reduce its emotional power over you.
- Affirmation: "I am in control of my thoughts. I can observe them from a distance without being consumed by them."

Practice Mindfulness Daily

- Exercise: Dedicate just five minutes a day to mindfulness. Sit quietly, breathe deeply, and focus on the present moment. If your mind wanders, gently bring it back to your breath or the present. Over time, increase the duration of your practice.

- Affirmation: "I am present in this moment. My mind is calm, clear, and focused."

**Readers' Notes:

Mantra for Daily Practice

Compete only with yourself, strive to be better than yesterday, and harness self-talk to stay motivated and chase your dreams.

Chapter 4

The Power of Intent

The same quiet evening. Kiritin sits alone, wrestling with his thoughts. Despite his external successes, an internal void gnaws at him. Sensing his inner turmoil, Kisan, his mentor and inner voice, appears to guide him. This dialogue draws inspiration from the profound teachings of the Bhagavad Gita, as Kisan, representing Krishna, helps Kiritin, embodying Arjuna, navigate his inner conflict.

Kiritin: (his voice strained with emotion) Kisan, I've done everything, followed every rule, checked every box. I've put in the long hours, climbed the corporate ladder, and reached the milestones. But here I am, standing at the top, and all I feel is... emptiness. Why do I feel so lost, despite everything I've achieved?

Kisan: (Stepping forward, his voice calm and soothing) Kiritin, you are facing a battle that many encounter but few conquer. You've been running a race, chasing goals laid out for you by others—by society, by expectations, by what you thought would bring you happiness. But these goals have been shaped by external influences, not by your true self. That is why you feel this void, this gnawing sense that something is missing. The difference between those who succeed and those who remain uncertain is their intent. The truly successful manifest their desires because they align their actions with a deep, personal intent. They don't just work hard; they work with purpose, gaining knowledge and experience along the way.

Kiritin: (shaking his head, confused) Intent? I've heard that word before, but it always seems so abstract. I thought success was the answer. I thought if I just worked hard enough, if I just achieved enough, I'd finally feel content and at peace. But now, all I feel is... empty. Like I've been climbing a ladder that's leaning against the wrong wall. How does intent really matter when you're just trying to make it in this world? Isn't hard work enough?

Kisan: (smiling gently) It's natural to feel lost when your actions aren't rooted in your true intent. Success—often defined superficially—can feel hollow if it's not tied to something deeper that resonates with who you truly are. The Bhagavad Gita teaches that the real value of our actions comes from the intent behind them, not just the outcomes. So, ask yourself, Kiritin: What drives you? What are the values at the core of your being? What vision do you have for your life, beyond the expectations of others?

Kiritin: (reflective) I... I've never really thought about that. I've been so focused on achieving that I've lost sight of why I'm doing any of this in the first place. My life has become a series of tasks and checkboxes. But I don't know what I truly stand for or what I really want. How do I even begin to uncover that?

Kisan: (patiently) Start by looking inward, Kiritin. Think about the moments in your life when you've felt truly alive, when your heart and mind were in perfect harmony. What were you doing then? What values were you honouring? Those moments are glimpses into your true self, into your core values. Your intent is born from these values. It's the "why" that gives meaning to the "what" and the "how."

Kiritin: (his voice softening) There was a time... I remember, back in college, I was struggling with my studies, trying to figure out who I was and why I was here. I felt so lost, like I was drowning in expectations—my own and everyone else's. I was doing everything I was supposed to do, but none of it felt right. It was like I was just going through the motions, without any real sense of purpose.

Kisan: (encouragingly) That experience was your soul's way of calling out to you, urging you to seek something deeper. At that moment, you were questioning the very foundation of your life—your purpose, your intent. It was a crucial turning point, Kiritin. You felt lost because you were living a life dictated by external desires rather than your own internal truth. But that feeling of being lost was also an opportunity, a chance to realign your actions with your true self.

Kiritin: (taking a deep breath, a sense of calm settling over him) Thank you, Kisan. I think I understand now. It's not about finding the perfect path—it's about finding my own path, one that aligns with my true self. And that path will reveal itself, step by step, as long as I stay true to my intent.

Kisan: (with a warm smile) That's right, Kiritin. Your intent will be your North Star, guiding you through the noise and distractions of the world. Regular self-reflection, meditation, and moments of stillness will help you stay grounded in your values and purpose. The Bhagavad Gita also teaches the importance of detachment—not from life, but from the outcomes of your actions. Focus on doing what feels right in your soul, and let go of the need for external validation. This way, you'll stay true to your path, no matter the challenges.

Kiritin: (with a sense of resolve) I'm ready, Kisan. I'm ready to realign my goals, my career, and my life with this newfound intent. I'll let my values guide me, and I'll trust in the process. I don't want to live with regrets. I want to look back on my life and know that I lived with purpose, that I acted with intent.

> *"Clarity of intent is the compass to your path. Without intent, you are like a phone without a signal—capable of much, but unable to connect to what matters."*

Kisan: (blessing him) May your journey be guided by your true intent, Kiritin. Remember, it's not the size of the task that defines its worth, but the intent behind it. When you live with intent, you fulfil your Dharma, and your life becomes an inspiration for others. This is the path to true success—a success that resonates with your soul and brings peace to your heart.

Kiritin: (with deep reflection) Thank you, Kisan. I feel like a weight has been lifted off my shoulders. I have a lot of work to do, but for the first time in a long time, I feel like I know where to start. Tonight, I'll begin—small steps, but with a clear purpose. I'll start living with intent, focusing on the journey, not just the destination.

Kisan: (with warmth and pride) That's the spirit, Kiritin. The first step is always the hardest, but with intent as your guide, every step will lead you closer to the fulfilment you seek. This is the beginning of a new chapter in your life—a chapter where your actions are guided by purpose and intent. Stay true to this path, and you will find the fulfilment you've been searching for. Remember, the journey is just as important as the destination. Now, go forth and manifest the life you truly desire, knowing that every step you take with intent is a step towards your true self.

 Action Step for Readers: Align Your Life with Your Intent

To fully embrace the power of intent and integrate the LIMIT Framework into your life, consider the following steps. These steps are designed to help you align your actions with your true purpose and live a more fulfilling, intentional life.

Reflect on Your Goals

- **Action**: Take a moment to sit quietly and list your current goals. For each goal, ask yourself, "Why is this important to me?" Delve beyond the surface reasons and explore whether these goals are driven by societal expectations or your genuine desires.
- **Example:** If your goal is to climb the corporate ladder, ask yourself why. Is it for financial stability, social status, or a genuine passion for the work? If the answer doesn't resonate with your core values, consider redefining the goal.

- **Affirmation:** "I set goals that reflect my true values and desires, not the expectations of others."

Identify Your True Intent

- **Action:** Reflect on the moments in your life when you felt most alive and fulfilled. What were you doing? Which values were you honouring? Write down these values and consider how they can guide your future decisions and actions.
- **Example:** If you felt truly alive while helping others, your true intent may involve service, compassion, or community. Use this insight to shape your goals and actions moving forward.
- **Affirmation:** "I understand my core values and allow them to guide my decisions and actions."

Realign Your Actions

- **Action:** Examine your daily activities, career, and lifestyle. Are they aligned with your identified intent? If not, consider what changes you can make to bring your life more in line with your true purpose. This might involve letting go of pursuits that do not resonate with your deeper values and focusing on those that do.
- **Example**: If your intent is rooted in creativity but your job feels stifling, look for ways to incorporate more creative tasks into your work or explore new career paths that align with this value.
- **Affirmation**: "I align my actions with my true intent, creating a life that reflects my deepest values."

Live with Purpose

- **Action**: Allow your intent to be the guiding force in your life. Let it influence your decisions, relationships, and daily actions. By living in alignment with your intent, you will experience greater clarity, fulfilment, and a sense of purpose.
- **Example**: If your intent is to build meaningful connections, prioritise quality time with loved ones, engage in deep conversations, and be present in your relationships. Let this intent guide how you interact with others.
- **Affirmation**: "I live each day with purpose, letting my true intent guide my decisions and actions."

Manifest Your Intent

- **Action**: Understand that manifestation is a continuous process. It requires you to think, plan, and work on your goals day and night. By consistently aligning your thoughts and actions with your intent, you bring your dreams into reality.
- **Example**: If you aspire to be a writer, set aside time each day to write, even if it's just a few sentences. Visualise your success and work towards it with dedication and passion.
- **Affirmation**: "I manifest my dreams by aligning my thoughts and actions with my true intent every day."

By following these steps, you can align your life with your true intent, creating a life that is not just about achieving external success but about fulfilling your deeper purpose and values.

This alignment leads to a more authentic, fulfilling existence and embodies the essence of the LIMIT Framework. It's about integrating your goals, actions, and daily life with your true self, ensuring that every step you take is guided by a meaningful, intentional purpose.

Readers' Notes:

 **Mantra for Daily Practice**

Figure out your 'Why': Why you're here, why you're doing this, and if it truly matters to you. Let your true intent, not societal expectations, drive your actions and give them meaning.

Chapter 5

Triggers and Responses

Kiritin sits by the edge of a quiet river, his mind restless with thoughts. The tranquillity of the scene starkly contrasts with the turmoil within him. Despite his achievements, he feels burdened by emotions that seem to control him at times. As he contemplates, Kisan, his inner mentor and guide, appears beside him, radiating calmness and wisdom.

Kiritin: Kisan, I feel lost. I've made progress, yet there are moments when a single word or action from someone can unravel me completely. I react without thinking, and afterwards, I'm left with regret. Why do I let these things affect me so deeply?

Kisan: Ah, Kiritin, your struggle is the struggle of many. The battlefield you face is not one of swords and shields but of the mind and heart. Like Arjuna, who stood confused and overwhelmed on the battlefield of Kurukshetra, you too are facing your internal war. These moments of intense reaction are your "triggers"—forces that provoke deep emotional responses. To gain mastery over them, you must understand their nature and learn to respond rather than react.

Kiritin: But Kisan, what are these triggers? Why do they have such power over me?

Kisan: Triggers are like arrows that pierce your heart, but the bow that releases them is often your own mind. They are tied to past experiences, unresolved emotions, and deep-seated fears. In the Bhagavad Gita, Krishna explains to Arjuna that our attachments and aversions are the true sources of suffering. Your triggers are linked to these attachments—whether to outcomes, the opinions of others, or your own expectations. When these attachments are threatened, the emotional storm within you is unleashed.

Kiritin: So, these triggers are not just random – they're rooted in my past and fears?

Kisan: Yes, Kiritin. Triggers can arise from many sources. A harsh word might remind you of past criticism, a failure could rekindle old fears of inadequacy, and a perceived rejection might reopen old wounds. These triggers bypass your conscious thought and strike directly at your heart, making you react impulsively. The key to overcoming them is recognising their nature and origin.

Kiritin: How can I manage these triggers? How can I prevent them from controlling me?

Kisan: You must cultivate awareness and develop strategies to cope with these triggers before they take root in your mind. In the Gita, Krishna guides Arjuna to still his mind and focus on his dharma—his true duty. Similarly, you must focus on your inner purpose and not be swayed by external forces. Consider these strategies:

- **Calling on Your Social Support:** Just as Arjuna sought counsel from Krishna, you must seek out those who can provide you with guidance and perspective. When you feel overwhelmed, reach out to someone you trust. They can help you see beyond the immediate emotion and remind you of your true path.
- **Deep Breathing:** In moments of emotional turmoil, pause and take deep breaths. This simple act can calm the storm within, giving you the space to respond wisely rather than react impulsively. The breath is your anchor, connecting you to the present moment.
- **Exercising:** Engage in physical activity to release the energy that builds up when you're triggered. Just as a warrior channels his energy into battle, you must channel your emotions into something constructive.
- **Expressive Writing:** When emotions overwhelm you, write them down. This allows you to process your feelings and gain clarity. By writing, you distance yourself from the immediate emotion, making it easier to reflect and respond.
- **Mindfulness Meditation:** Practice mindfulness to stay present. When you observe your thoughts without judgment, you prevent them from controlling you. Mindfulness is the art of witnessing your emotions without becoming entangled in them.

Kiritin: These strategies sound powerful, Kisan, but how will I know if I'm truly responding instead of just reacting?

Kisan: The difference lies in intention and awareness, Kiritin. Reacting is impulsive, driven by the emotional brain. It is an immediate action that often leads to regret. Responding, however, involves a pause—a moment to reflect and choose a course of action that aligns with your values and goals. In the Bhagavad Gita, Krishna teaches that self-mastery begins with mastering the mind. By responding thoughtfully, you take control of your actions and, ultimately, your destiny.

Kiritin: And what impact does responding have on my life compared to reacting?

Kisan: Reacting is a chain that binds you to your past and perpetuates cycles of regret. It's like being a puppet controlled by the strings of your emotions. Responding, however, is an act of liberation. It breaks the chain, allowing you to grow and evolve. In the Gita, Krishna teaches that through self-awareness and disciplined action, one can rise above the turmoil of the mind and achieve true peace. When you respond with clarity and purpose, you transform every challenge into an opportunity for growth.

Kiritin: (his voice trembling with emotion) Kisan, I don't understand. I've been working so hard, trying to stay focused and positive, but it feels like every time I start to make progress, something happens—a word, a look, a small setback—and I lose control. I react without thinking, and afterward, I'm left feeling ashamed and confused. Why do I let these things affect me so deeply? Why can't I stay strong in the face of challenges?

Kisan: (with a calm, knowing smile) Ah, Kiritin, what you're experiencing is something many face on their journey. The challenges you encounter are not just tests of your external abilities but also of your inner strength and resilience. Life, you see, is a series of transformations, each marked by a certain degree of pain. From the moment you are born to the moment you die, and through every significant change in between, there is always a price to be paid – a struggle, a sacrifice. It's through this pain that true success and growth are achieved.

Kiritin: (confused, searching for clarity) But why must everything start with pain, Kisan? Can't there be a path to success that isn't so difficult?

Kisan: (thoughtfully) Pain, Kiritin, is the universe's way of shaping you, of refining your character. Consider this: gold is purified in the hottest of fires, and a rough stone is meticulously carved to become a revered idol. Just as these elements undergo intense processes to reveal their true beauty and value, you, too, are being shaped by the challenges you face. Adversity is not your enemy—it is your greatest opportunity for growth. It's the pressure that turns coal into diamonds, the struggle that makes you stronger.

Kiritin: (reflecting) So, the hardships I'm going through are meant to make me better, not break me?

Kisan: Exactly. But it's not just about enduring adversity; it's about how you handle it. There's a critical difference between reacting to a situation and responding to it. Reacting is often impulsive, driven by the immediate emotions of the moment—your likes, dislikes, and your ego. Responding, on the other hand, is a deliberate, thoughtful action. It's the difference between recklessly shooting an arrow and carefully aiming before you release it. Once an arrow is shot, it cannot be retrieved, just as your reactions cannot be undone once they are out in the world.

Kiritin: (sighing deeply) I understand, but in the heat of the moment, it's so hard to control my reactions. How can I prevent these triggers from taking over and affecting me so deeply?

Kisan:(with wisdom) Think of your mind as a bow, and your thoughts and emotions as the arrows. When you draw the bowstring, you gather energy, focus, and intention. But if you release it carelessly, the arrow may miss its target or cause unintended harm. Your mind works in the same way—when tension builds within you, whether from fear, anger, or frustration, you must learn to control it before it is unleashed. Like tuning a radio or television to the right frequency, you must tune your mind to a higher state of awareness, where external words and actions cannot disturb your inner peace.

Kiritin: (curious, leaning in) What do you mean by tuning my mind to a higher state? How do I do that?

Kisan: (nodding) It's about recognising that the power to affect you lies not in the external circumstances, but in how you perceive and react to them. Just as wood has the potential for fire within it, you have the potential for greatness within you. The key is to ignite that potential in a way that fuels your growth rather than consumes you. When someone says something that triggers you, for example, instead of reacting immediately, pause. Take a deep breath. This act of pausing is like a spark that can ignite your inner fire in a controlled, purposeful way.

> *"A gift not accepted remains with the giver. Be the gatekeeper of your mind; the only force that can influence you is yourself."*

Kiritin: (thoughtful) So, I must learn to respond rather than react, to channel my inner fire and direct it with intention?

Kisan: Yes, Kiritin. Begin by focusing on learning from every experience, whether it brings success or failure. Celebrate the wisdom you gain rather than the outcome itself. Life is a continuous process of learning, and each moment, whether joyful or painful, offers a lesson. When you approach life with this mindset, your reactions will gradually transform into thoughtful responses.

Kiritin: (with renewed resolve) I see now, Kisan. My journey is not just about external success, but about mastering my inner world. I must learn to control my reactions, to respond with intention, and embrace every challenge as an opportunity to grow.

Kisan: (with warmth and encouragement) That's the spirit, Kiritin. Remember, the fire within you is powerful. When you harness it with wisdom and intent, you can achieve greatness. Focus on learning from every experience, celebrate your growth, and let go of the need for immediate success. With time and practice, your reactions will transform into purposeful responses, and you will find a peace that cannot be shaken by the world around you.

Kiritin: (with a thoughtful expression) Thank you, Kisan. I've realised that my reactions to triggers have often clouded my judgement and led to regret. I recall an instance when I received critical feedback, and instead of taking it constructively, I reacted defensively. This pattern has been a recurring issue for me.

Kisan: (nodding) That's a significant realisation, Kiritin. Let's explore this further. Share more about how you reacted to that feedback. What was your initial response, and how did it affect you?

Kiritin: (reflecting) When I received the feedback, I felt an immediate surge of frustration. I thought my work was solid, and the criticism felt like a personal attack. I responded by arguing and trying to justify my actions, which only made the situation worse. I didn't realise at the time that this response was driven by my ego and my fear of failure. Looking back, I see that the feedback was actually valuable, but my reaction prevented me from seeing its true worth.

Kisan: (compassionately) It's natural to feel defensive when faced with criticism, but understanding the nature of your response can lead to growth. Remember, as Krishna teaches Arjuna in the Bhagavad Gita, our reactions are often driven by our attachments and fears. To transform these reactions into opportunities for growth, you must first become aware of them.

Kiritin: (curiously) How can I start transforming my reactions into more thoughtful responses?

Kisan: (with clarity) Start by identifying situations that trigger strong emotional reactions, as you did with the feedback. Keep a journal to document these triggers and your immediate responses. This will help you recognise patterns and understand the root causes of your reactions.

Kiritin: (nodding) That makes sense. I can see how identifying these triggers might help me understand my reactions better.

Kiritin feels a profound sense of clarity and purpose. The river before him flows gently, and he knows that, like the river, his journey will have twists and turns. But with awareness and intention, he can navigate them with grace.

 Action Steps for Readers

Begin by identifying situations, people, or thoughts that trigger strong emotional reactions in you. Keep a journal to document these triggers and your immediate responses. Practice deep breathing and mindfulness techniques to create a pause between the trigger and your response. Reflect on your reactions and consciously choose to respond in a way that aligns with your values and long-term goals. The following steps are designed to guide you on a journey of self-mastery, helping you turn your emotional triggers into powerful catalysts for growth and resilience.

Identify Your Triggers

- **Exercise:** Pay close attention to situations, people, or thoughts that provoke strong emotional reactions within you. These could range from a critical comment from a colleague to a stressful situation at home.
- **Affirmation:**
  "I am aware of my triggers and acknowledge their impact on my emotions."
- **Action:** Keep a journal where you document each trigger as it occurs. Note what exactly caused the reaction, how

you felt, and your immediate response. This practice will help you identify patterns and gain a deeper understanding of your emotional landscape.

Practice the Pause

- **Exercise:** Whenever you feel a strong emotion rising, pause for a moment. Instead of reacting immediately, take a deep breath and focus on calming your mind.
- **Affirmation:**
  "I choose to pause and breathe deeply before responding to any situation."
- **Action:** Incorporate deep breathing exercises into your daily routine. For instance, try taking five slow, deep breaths whenever you feel triggered. This will create a space between the stimulus and your response, allowing you to approach the situation with clarity.

Reflect on Your Reactions

- **Exercise:** After each emotional event, take some time to reflect on how you reacted. Were your actions in line with your values and long-term goals? If not, consider how you could have responded differently.
- **Affirmation:**
  "I reflect on my reactions with compassion and strive to align them with my true self."
- **Action:** Use your journal to record your reflections. Ask yourself: "What was I feeling in that moment?" "Why did I react the way I did?" "How could I respond more mindfully next time?" This reflection will help you learn from each experience and gradually shift from reactive to responsive behaviour.

Consciously Choose Your Response

- **Exercise:** In moments of emotional intensity, consciously choose how you want to respond. Consider your values and long-term goals before taking action.
- **Affirmation:**
  "I choose my responses consciously, aligning them with my core values and aspirations."
- **Action:** Before responding to a trigger, ask yourself: "Is this reaction in line with who I want to be?" "Does this response serve my long-term goals?" "How can I turn this situation into a growth opportunity?" This will help you make decisions that are thoughtful and purposeful.

Transform Triggers into Growth

- **Exercise:** View each trigger as an opportunity to grow and strengthen your emotional resilience. Celebrate small victories when you respond thoughtfully rather than react impulsively.
- **Affirmation:**
  "I transform my triggers into powerful opportunities for personal growth and resilience."
- **Action:** Each time you successfully manage a trigger, acknowledge your progress. Reflect on how this shift has positively impacted your emotional stability and resilience. Over time, what once felt like a vulnerability will serve as a source of strength and growth.

Cultivate Mindfulness and Presence

- **Exercise:** Regularly practise mindfulness meditation to stay grounded in the present moment. This will help you become more aware of your thoughts and emotions as they arise, allowing you to respond rather than react.

- **Affirmation:**
  "I live in the present moment, aware of my thoughts and emotions, and respond with wisdom and grace."
- **Action:** Set aside a few minutes each day for mindfulness meditation. During this time, focus on your breath, observe your thoughts without judgment, and allow yourself to simply be present. This practice will strengthen your ability to maintain composure and clarity, even in the face of triggering situations.

Celebrate Your Progress

- **Exercise:** Regularly acknowledge and celebrate your progress in managing your emotional triggers. Recognise how far you've come in transforming these challenges into opportunities for growth.
- **Affirmation:**
  "I celebrate my progress and honour the journey of personal growth and resilience."
- **Action:** At the end of each week or month, review your journal and reflect on the progress you've made. Celebrate the moments where you responded with intention and set goals for continued growth. This positive reinforcement will motivate you to keep moving forward on your path of self-mastery.

By integrating these steps into your daily life, you will begin to see your emotional triggers not as obstacles, but as powerful opportunities for personal development. Over time, you'll cultivate greater emotional stability, resilience, and inner peace, aligning your responses with your highest self and long-term aspirations.

Readers' Notes:

 Mantra for Daily Practice

Consciously choose to respond, not react, and turn
emotional triggers into catalysts for growth
and resilience.

Limit Framework Playbook

A Printable Quick Reference

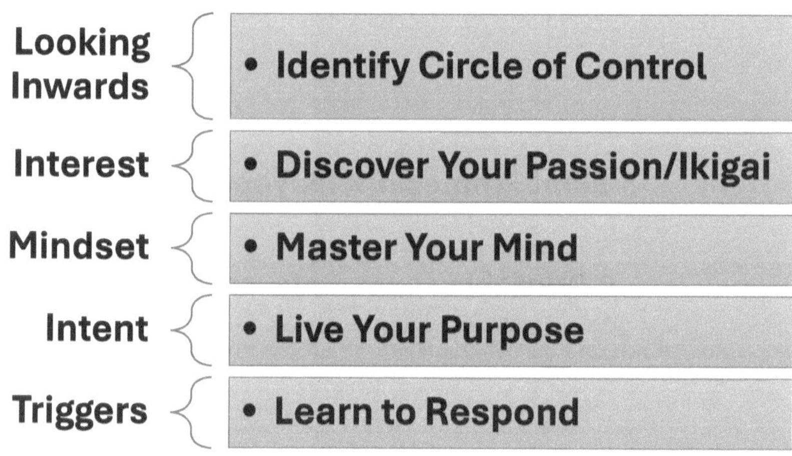

Looking Inwards
Interest
Mindset
Intent
Triggers
• Identify Circle of Control
• Discover Your Passion/Ikigai
• Master Your Mind
• Live Your Purpose
• Learn to Respond

Part II

Chapter 6

The Crossroads

FOLLOWING DREAMS OR PLAYING IT SAFE?

Imagine standing at the crossroads of your life, facing two paths. One leads to the safety of what you know—your current life, predictable and secure. The other is the road of your dreams—unmapped, filled with uncertainty, but calling to you with the promise of something greater. Which path will you choose? The comfort of the known or the excitement of the unknown?

As you reflect on your journey, ask yourself: Has the LIMIT Framework guided me in following my dreams? Consider each aspect:

- **Have I Known My Limits**, understanding what I can control and what I must surrender?
- **Have I Known My Interest**, aligning my pursuits with what truly ignites my passion?
- **Have I Known My Mind**, harnessing my thoughts to drive positive change?
- **Have I Known My Intent**, grounding my actions in a purpose that's deeply personal and true to me?
- **Have I Known My Trigger**, recognizing and managing the emotional reactions that could hold me back?

Confront Your Fears

Fear often lurks at these crossroads, whispering doubts. It asks, "What if I fail? What if I'm not good enough? What if I lose everything?" These fears, though valid, are only as powerful as you allow them to be. Ask yourself: Am I truly living or merely existing? Are you moving forward, driven by passion and purpose, or are you simply going through the motions, confined by comfort and convention?

Align Your Intent with Your Dreams

Does the voice of Kisan—your inner guide—echo in your mind, reminding you of the importance of knowing your intent? This principle isn't just about setting goals; it's about understanding why those goals matter. When your intent is clear, it becomes a compass, directing you towards a life that's not just lived but truly meaningful. Are you aligning your intent with your dreams, or are you letting the expectations of others dictate your path?

Embrace Your True Desires

To follow your dreams, you must be willing to embrace your true desires, trust in the process, and let go of the need for external validation. Consider this: If you stripped away all the expectations of society, family, and peers, what would remain? What do you truly want? Are you pursuing your dreams because they are yours, or because they fit neatly into the picture others have painted for you?

Live a Life of Purpose

Following your dreams isn't just a choice; it's a necessity for living a life of purpose. A life guided by intent is one where every action, no matter how small, contributes to something greater – a vision that's uniquely yours.

Reflection Point

- What dreams have you been holding back on, and why?
- How does fear influence your decisions, and what would you do differently if fear were not a factor?
- When was the last time you felt truly alive, and what were you doing?
- What does success look like for you, and is it aligned with your deepest desires or others' expectations?
- What small step can you take today to move closer to your dreams?
- If you were to let go of external validation, how would your life change?
- In what ways can you align your daily actions more closely with your true intent?

Action Step for Readers: Embrace the Challenge

Ask yourself

1. What do I truly desire? Reflect on your deepest aspirations. Write them down and be honest with yourself.
2. What's holding me back? Identify the fears and external pressures that keep you from pursuing your dreams. Challenge these obstacles head-on.
3. Am I living according to my true intent? Evaluate whether your current path aligns with your core values and long-term vision. If it doesn't, what needs to change?

4. What first step can I take today? Start small, but take action. The journey of a thousand miles begins with a single step.

5. The road less travelled is daunting, but it's also where you find your greatest growth, fulfilment, and legacy. Trust in your inner Kisan, let the LIMIT Framework guide you, and take that courageous step towards a life that is truly yours.

Readers' Notes:

THE TURNING POINT

There comes a time in every journey when you find yourself at the crossroads—a moment when the choice before you is not just a decision but a chance to break free, to liberate yourself from the chains that have held you back. This is your turning point. It is not merely a shift in direction; it is a powerful, transformative moment that redefines who you are and what you are capable of becoming.

But what will you choose?

The Stagnation of Playing It Safe

Do you find yourself clinging to the familiar, hoping that safety will protect you from the uncertainty of the unknown? Reflect deeply on your past choices. Have they led to growth, or have they merely preserved a status quo that no longer serves you? The illusion of security can often be a prison in disguise, keeping you locked away from your true potential.

When you look back on your life, does the voice of Kisan, your inner mentor, whisper in your mind that playing it safe has only led to stagnation? Does the LIMIT Framework not urge you to break through these self-imposed barriers? This framework isn't just about identifying limits; it's about shattering them, pushing past what you once thought was possible.

The Realization of Self-Imposed Constraints

Can you see how many of your limitations are not real but self-imposed? How many times have you let doubt, fear, or the expectations of others dictate your choices? The walls around you are not made of stone; they are constructed from the beliefs you've built within your own mind. Kisan's voice reminds you that these beliefs can be dismantled, and the only true barriers are the ones you allow to stand.

What will it take for you to recognise that your limits are illusions? Will this be the moment you decide to challenge the narratives that have held you captive? This realisation is the catalyst for change, the spark that ignites the fire of transformation.

Embracing the Unknown

At this crossroads, the road ahead is not lined with certainty. It is filled with risks, challenges, and the unknown. But it is also filled with the promise of growth, discovery, and a life lived on your terms. What will you choose? Will you remain bound by the fear of the unknown, or will you break free, trusting that the journey ahead holds the fulfilment you've been searching for?

Reflection Point

- When you reflect on your journey, do you see moments where you chose safety over growth? How did that choice shape your life, and are you satisfied with where it led?
- What self-imposed limits have held you back? Can you identify the beliefs that have kept you from embracing your true potential?
- Does the voice of Kisan echo in your mind, urging you to step beyond your comfort zone? How does this realization shift your perspective on your current challenges?
- Are you ready to confront the fears that have shackled you? What would it feel like to finally embrace the unknown and claim the life you've always dreamed of?

Action Step for Readers: A Moment of Liberation

Ask yourself: Reflect on a moment in your life when you chose to play it safe. Write down the reasons why you made that choice and how it affected your journey. Then, identify a current situation where you are tempted to play it safe again. Challenge yourself to make a different choice this time—one that aligns with your true desires, even if it means stepping into the unknown. Commit to taking one bold action that pushes you past your perceived limits. Let this be your turning point, the moment where you choose liberation over fear, growth over stagnation.

Readers' Notes:

NEWFOUND CLARITY AND SUPPORT

There comes a time in every journey when the fog lifts, revealing a path that was always there but hidden from view. This is your moment of clarity, a revelation so profound that it redefines your understanding of self, purpose, and the universe around you. With this newfound clarity, do you feel a deep sense of support from the very universe that once seemed indifferent? Have you noticed how the world now mirrors your inner state, reflecting your thoughts, beliefs, and intentions?

This clarity isn't just intellectual – it's transformative. It's as if the universe itself has shifted to align with your purpose. The support you once sought externally, from people, circumstances, or opportunities, was never truly out there. It was within you all along, waiting patiently to be recognised. Now, as you stand on this newfound ground, do you realise that the clarity you've gained is more than just an understanding? It's a call to live authentically, to embrace your true self, and to trust that when your intent is pure, the universe conspires to support you.

But this clarity also brings responsibility. It asks you to question: Are you prepared to step forward with this new awareness, to live in alignment with your highest self? Will you dare to trust the process, to let go of doubts and fears, and to embrace the path that is uniquely yours?

 **Action Step for Readers**

Pause and reflect on your own journey. With this newfound clarity, ask yourself: What is the universe showing me about my true path? Write down the moments when you've felt a deep sense of inner support and identify how you can align your daily actions with this clarity. Trust that the support you seek is already within you, waiting for you to acknowledge it. Take a bold step forward, knowing that with clarity and intent, the universe is on your side.

Readers' Notes:

Chapter 7

Embracing Change

Change is Inevitable

Change is inevitable. It sweeps through our lives like a storm, uprooting comfort zones, challenging established norms, and pushing us toward new horizons. But within this storm lies the power to redefine who we are and to rewrite the story of our lives. Through the lens of the LIMIT Framework, embracing change becomes not just a necessity but a powerful journey of transformation. Let's delve into how we can redefine success, find the courage to pursue our passions, and understand the ripple effect of our choices.

<u>REDEFINING SUCCESS</u>

Kiritin: "Kisan, I've always believed that success means reaching the top—having wealth, recognition, and power. But lately, I've felt empty, as if I'm chasing a dream that isn't mine. How do I find success that truly fulfils me?"

Kisan: "Success, Kiritin, is not a destination; it's an evolving journey that mirrors your growth and inner transformation. The world defines success in terms of wealth, status, and power, but these are fleeting. What if true success lies in aligning your actions with your deepest values and passions? Imagine the peace that comes from living authentically, from knowing that your life reflects who you truly are. Can you redefine success to fit this vision? How would it change the way you live?"

Reflection Point

- How do you currently define success, and what impact has this definition had on your life?
- If you could redefine success based solely on your values and passions, what would it look like?
- What steps can you take today to start living in alignment with this new definition?

Why It's Important to Embrace Change by Redefining Success

Success is often perceived as a fixed endpoint—a peak we strive to reach. But what happens when we achieve it, only to realise it doesn't bring the fulfilment we expected? Redefining success allows us to shift our focus from external validation to internal alignment. It's crucial because it frees us from societal pressures, enabling us to pursue a life that truly resonates with who we are. This change empowers us to live authentically, making decisions that bring long-term joy and peace rather than momentary satisfaction.

Action Step for Readers

Reflect on your current definition of success. Is it based on societal expectations or personal fulfilment? Rewrite your definition to align with your core values and long-term goals, embracing it as a dynamic, evolving journey rather than a fixed point.

Readers' Notes:

<u>COURAGE TO PURSUE YOUR PASSION</u>

Kiritin: "Kisan, I've always had a passion, but fear holds me back. What if I fail? What if it leads nowhere? How do I find the courage to follow my heart when the risks seem so high?"

Kisan: "Courage, Kiritin, is not the absence of fear but the strength to act despite it. Your passion is the fire within you—ignoring it is the greatest risk of all. Imagine living a life where you never pursued your dreams, where you played it safe but felt unfulfilled. How does that feel? What if the path less travelled is the one that leads to your true purpose? How can you start pursuing your passion today, even if it's just a small step?"

Reflection Point

- What passion have you buried due to fear, and how has this affected your sense of fulfilment?
- If fear weren't holding you back, what passion would you pursue, and why?
- What small step can you take today to begin following your passion?

Why It's Important to Embrace Change by Having the Courage to Pursue Your Passion

Passion is the heartbeat of a fulfilled life. Yet, pursuing it often requires stepping into the unknown, breaking away from the safety of the familiar. This is where courage becomes essential. Embracing change through courage allows us to pursue our passions, even when the path is uncertain. It's important because living without passion leads to a life of regret and unfulfilled potential. By pursuing what truly matters to us, we ignite a sense of purpose that fuels our growth and happiness.

 Action Step for Readers

Identify a passion you've been hesitant to pursue. Write down the fears and obstacles holding you back. Then, outline a small, actionable step you can take towards embracing this passion. Remember, courage is built one step at a time.

Readers' Notes:

<u>THE RIPPLE EFFECT</u>

Kiritin: "Kisan, I'm just one person. How can my choices and actions really make a difference? I feel so insignificant sometimes, like what I do doesn't matter."

Kisan: "Never underestimate the power of a single drop, Kiritin. Every action you take sends ripples into the world, touching lives in ways you may never see. Reflect on this: How have others' choices shaped your life? Now, consider the impact your choices could have on others. When you live authentically and pursue your passion, you inspire those around you to do the same. What kind of ripple do you want to create? How will your actions today shape the future?"

Reflection Point

- Who has influenced your life through their actions, and how did it change you?
- What impact do you want to have on others through your choices and actions?
- How can you consciously create positive ripples in your everyday life?

Why It's Important to Embrace Change by Understanding the Ripple Effect

Our actions, no matter how small, have the power to influence others. Embracing change through the ripple effect is important because it reminds us that we are part of a larger whole. The courage to pursue our passion, the decision to redefine success—these choices don't just change our lives; they inspire others to reflect and grow. By living authentically, we create a positive impact that extends far beyond ourselves.

Understanding the ripple effect empowers us to be intentional with our actions, knowing that we have the power to influence the world for the better.

 Action Step for Readers

Reflect on a time when someone else's actions positively influenced you. Consider how your current actions could be creating ripples in the lives of others. Identify one area in your life where you can be a positive influence and take deliberate action to create a ripple effect that aligns with your values.

Readers' Notes:

Conclusion: Embrace the Storm

Change is like standing in the eye of a storm—chaotic yet full of potential. By redefining success, finding the courage to pursue your passion, and understanding the ripple effect of your actions, you harness this storm's power to transform your life. The LIMIT Framework is your compass on this journey, guiding you to live authentically and fully, not just for yourself but for those around you.

Now is the time to take action. Reflect, redefine, and reimagine what your life could be. The storm is here—embrace it and let it propel you to new heights.

Chapter 8

Integrating the Framework

Integrating the LIMIT Framework: A Deeper Journey

The LIMIT Framework is a powerful guide designed to help you understand yourself, navigate life's challenges, and live a life aligned with your true purpose. However, the framework reaches its full potential only when integrated into your daily life. To truly transform, you must move from understanding the concepts to living them every day. Let's explore the lessons learned, how to apply the "Know Your Limit Framework" in daily life, and the final words of wisdom that resonate through your inner voice, just as Kiritin was guided by Kisan.

LESSONS LEARNED: THE PATH TO WISDOM

Kiritin: "Kisan, looking back, I see how much I've grown. But what do these lessons mean for my future? How do I ensure I carry them with me?"

Kisan: "Kiritin, each lesson you've learned is a piece of the puzzle that makes you whole. The framework has taught you more than just concepts—it has given you tools for life. The real question is, what will you do with these lessons? Will you let them gather dust, or will you use them to shape your future? Remember, wisdom is not just in knowing; it's in applying what you know. How will you let these lessons guide you as you move forward?"

Reflection Point

- What lessons have you learned from your journey so far? Have they changed the way you see the world, or are they simply memories?
- How often do you reflect on these lessons when making decisions?
- Are there lessons you've learned but haven't yet fully embraced? What's holding you back from living by them?

The lessons within the LIMIT Framework are not just intellectual exercises – they are essential to your growth. Each lesson teaches you about yourself: your strengths, weaknesses, passions, and boundaries. But the real power lies in applying these lessons. Learning without action is empty; it's the daily application that turns lessons into wisdom. Embracing these lessons is vital because they serve as the foundation for a life of purpose, authenticity, and fulfilment.

 ## Action Step for Readers

Choose one lesson from your life that you feel has the potential to transform you but hasn't yet been fully integrated. Reflect on why it's important and commit to applying it in your daily life for the next 30 days. Notice how this small change influences your mindset, decisions, and overall well-being.

Readers' Notes:

APPLYING THE "LIMIT FRAMEWORK" IN DAILY LIFE: LIVING WITH INTENTION

Kiritin: "Kisan, it's one thing to understand the framework, but how do I make it a part of who I am? How do I ensure that it guides my everyday life?"

Kisan: "The LIMIT Framework isn't just for the big moments; it's for every moment. It's about waking up each day with a clear sense of who you are and what you want to achieve. Start by knowing your limits—what will you focus on today, and what will you let go of? Then, align your actions with your interests—how will you infuse passion into your work? Shape your mindset—what thoughts will you choose to nurture? Clarify your intent—what's driving your actions today? And finally, be aware of your triggers—how will you manage your emotions and reactions? The framework is your daily guide, your roadmap to a life lived with purpose and intention. But it's only as effective as you allow it to be. How will you live it today?"

Reflection Point

- How often do you start your day with a clear intention, knowing exactly what you want to achieve?
- Do you regularly set boundaries that protect your energy and focus, or do you let the demands of the day dictate your actions?
- When challenges arise, do you react out of habit, or do you pause to consider your triggers and choose a mindful response?
- What would happen if you began each day by consciously applying the LIMIT Framework?

Life is a series of moments, and it's in these moments that true change occurs. The LIMIT Framework is designed to be lived, not just understood. When you apply it daily, you stay aligned with your values, passions, and purpose. It becomes easier to make decisions, navigate challenges, and remain true to yourself. This framework transforms ordinary days into extraordinary opportunities for growth and fulfilment, guiding you toward your highest potential.

 Action Step for Readers

Create a morning routine that includes a brief reflection on the LIMIT Framework. Spend a few minutes considering your limits, interests, mindset, intent, and triggers for the day. Set clear intentions and make a plan to apply the framework throughout your day. At the end of the day, reflect on how well you lived in alignment with your intentions and adjust as needed.

Readers' Notes:

FINAL WORDS OF WISDOM: TRUSTING YOUR INNER VOICE

Kiritin: "Kisan, your guidance has been invaluable, but how do I continue on this path when I face doubts and fears? How do I find the strength to keep going?"

Kisan: "Kiritin, my guidance was never about giving you answers—it was about helping you find your own. You see, the voice you've heard all along was not mine but your own inner wisdom. The LIMIT Framework was a mirror reflecting the truths you already knew. When doubts and fears arise, remember this: you have everything you need within you. Trust your inner voice, for it knows your path better than anyone else. It's the voice that understands your limits, that aligns with your interests, that shapes your mind, clarifies your intent, and recognises your triggers. The journey ahead will not always be easy, but you will never be alone. Your inner voice is always with you, guiding you, just as I have. Can you hear it now, guiding you even through the noise of the world?"

Reflection Point

- When was the last time you truly listened to your inner voice? Did it guide you towards something meaningful, or did you ignore it?
- How often do you silence your inner wisdom in favour of external advice, even when it doesn't resonate with your values?
- What would change in your life if you started trusting yourself more, just as Kiritin trusted Kisan?

Your inner voice is the essence of who you are—it's the culmination of your experiences, values, and intuition. It's the voice that aligns you with your true purpose, even when the world tries to lead you astray. Trusting your inner voice is vital because it's your most authentic guide. It's not influenced by societal pressures or external expectations; it speaks only the truth of who you are and what you need. By listening to it, you live a life that is true to yourself, one that is guided by wisdom, not fear.

 Action Step for Readers

The next time you face a decision, take a moment to sit quietly and listen to your inner voice. What is it telling you? Write down what you hear and commit to acting on this guidance, even if it feels challenging or unconventional. Trust that your inner voice knows what's best for you, just as Kiritin learned to trust Kisan.

Readers' Notes:

◎ Conclusion: The Challenge to Fully Integrate

The LIMIT Framework is a powerful tool, but it's only as effective as your commitment to live by it. The lessons you've learned, the daily application of the framework, and the wisdom of your inner voice are all parts of this journey. But they require action—consistent, intentional action. The challenge now is to integrate the framework fully into your life, to let it guide you in every decision, every interaction, and every step forward. Embrace the journey, trust yourself, and let the LIMIT Framework be your guide to a life of purpose, authenticity, and fulfilment.

Remember, the true journey is not just about reaching a destination, but about living each day with intention and heart. Now, take the first step – integrate, live, and become the person you were always meant to be.

Chapter 9

A New Beginning

A Journey Guided by the LIMIT Framework

A new beginning is more than a fresh start—it's a profound transformation, an invitation to explore the depths of who you are and who you can become. Within this journey lies the essence of the LIMIT Framework, which serves as a guiding compass, leading you toward a life that resonates with authenticity, passion, and balance. As you embark on this path, know that the voice within you—your inner guide—is waiting to be heard. Like Kiritin in *Limits Unleashed*, a mentor like Kisan will come when you need them most. This new beginning calls you to align with your true interests, celebrate the courage it takes to pursue your passions, and cultivate a balanced life that allows for continued growth.

ALIGNING WITH YOUR TRUE INTERESTS

In today's world, it's easy to find yourself entangled in expectations—whether imposed by society, family, or even yourself. The pursuit of goals that aren't truly yours can lead to frustration, burnout, and a sense of emptiness. Aligning with your true interests, however, is the key to unlocking a life of meaning and fulfilment. It's about tuning out the noise and listening to the quiet but persistent voice inside that knows what you truly desire.

Kiritin, like many of us, struggled with the expectations of others. He was driven by what he thought he should do, not by what he wanted to do. His turning point came when he chose to listen to his inner voice—a voice that had been there all along, waiting for him to acknowledge it. With Kisan's guidance, Kiritin realised that true success wasn't about fulfilling others' dreams but about pursuing his own. By aligning with his true interests, he not only found joy and purpose but also a renewed sense of energy and enthusiasm for life.

Ask yourself: What truly interests you? What activities or pursuits make you lose track of time and feel most alive? Are you following a path that aligns with these interests, or are you chasing goals that don't resonate with who you are? What would your life look like if you fully embraced your passions?

🤝 Action Step for Readers

Reflect on your true interests. Write down one interest or passion that you've neglected. Commit to dedicating time and energy to it, even if it's just a small step. Remember, aligning with your true interests is the foundation of a fulfilling life, and every small step counts.

Readers' Notes:

A CELEBRATION OF COURAGE

Courage is the force that propels us to step out of the shadows of fear and into the light of possibility. It's the strength to pursue what sets our hearts on fire, even when the path is uncertain and the outcome unknown. But courage doesn't always come easily – it's something we build, one step at a time, by confronting our fears and choosing to act despite them.

Kiritin's journey required immense courage. He had to face not only his fears but also the doubts and scepticism of those around him. It would have been easier to stay in his comfort zone, to follow the path others had set for him. But Kiritin knew that comfort without fulfilment would leave him empty. Encouraged by Kisan, he found the strength to pursue his passion, even when the way forward seemed daunting. This courage wasn't about being fearless—it was about being willing to act in the presence of fear. With each courageous step, Kiritin grew stronger, more confident, and more aligned with his true self.

Ask yourself: What fear is holding you back from pursuing your passion? What would it take for you to overcome this fear? When was the last time you acted courageously, and how did it change you? How can you celebrate your own acts of courage, no matter how small?

 ## Action Step for Readers

Identify one area in your life where you need to summon more courage. It could be as simple as expressing your true feelings, taking a risk on a new venture, or saying no to something that no longer serves you. Take that step today. Courage is a muscle – the more you use it, the stronger it becomes.

Readers' Notes:

A BALANCED LIFE: CONTINUED GROWTH

Life is a delicate balance between striving and being, between ambition and peace. When we focus too much on one and neglect the other, we lose the harmony that sustains us. A balanced life is not about perfection but about continuous growth—allowing yourself to evolve while also making time for rest, reflection, and renewal.

In *Limits Unleashed*, Kiritin learned the importance of balance through Kisan's wisdom. He discovered that pushing himself too hard without pause led to burnout, while too much rest without ambition left him unfulfilled. True growth, Kisan taught him, happens when we find a rhythm that honours both our drive to achieve and our need for peace. This balance allowed Kiritin to grow not just in his pursuits but also in his understanding of himself. He realized that life's greatest achievements come from doing what truly matters. It's about approaching those moments with intention and mindfulness.

Ask yourself: Are you living a balanced life? Do you make time for reflection and renewal, or are you constantly on the go? How can you create a routine that honours both your ambitions and your need for peace? What does continued growth look like for you—not just in what you achieve, but in who you become?

🤝 Action Step for Readers

Reflect on your current balance between work and rest, action and reflection. Identify one area where you feel out of sync. It might be your work-life balance, your mental and physical health, or your emotional well-being. Take a step towards restoring balance, whether it's setting boundaries, prioritising self-care, or simply allowing yourself to be present. Growth is not just about moving forward—it's about knowing when to pause and recalibrate.

Readers' Notes:

🎯 Conclusion: Embrace Your New Beginning

A new beginning is a profound gift—a chance to realign, to step into your courage, and to create a balanced life that allows for continued growth. The LIMIT Framework offers you the tools to navigate this journey, guiding you to listen to your inner voice and trust that a mentor like Kisan will appear when you need them most. As you stand at the threshold of this new chapter, remember: the journey is yours to create. Align with your true interests, celebrate your courage, and cultivate a life that balances ambition with peace. Your new beginning is not just about what you do—it's about who you become along the way. Listen, trust, and take the first step. The path awaits you.

Conclusion

The Road Ahead

The road ahead is not a simple, straightforward path. It is winding, unpredictable, and often fraught with challenges that will test your resolve. But within these challenges lies the opportunity for growth and transformation. As you move forward, it's essential to remember that failure is not just a possibility; it's a certainty. But so too is your capacity to rise again, stronger and more determined. The LIMIT Framework is your compass on this journey—a set of guiding principles that will help you navigate the storms, find your direction, and ultimately achieve fulfilment.

RECAP OF THE KEY PRINCIPLES OF THE FRAMEWORK

The LIMIT Framework is a holistic approach to self-discovery and growth. Each principle is a piece of the puzzle that, when put together, creates a clear picture of who you are and who you can become.

- **Know Your Limits by Looking Inward:** The first step is understanding where your boundaries lie. These limits are not meant to confine you but to help you recognise where growth is needed. Knowing your limits is about self-awareness—understanding what you can control, where you can push further, and when to seek help or change course.

- **Know Your Interests:** Life is too short to live for anything other than what you are passionate about. Aligning your actions with your interests ensures that your journey is one of fulfilment and joy. This principle encourages you to pursue what makes you feel alive and to follow the sparks of curiosity that light up your soul.

- **Know Your Mind:** Your mindset is the lens through which you view the world. A positive, growth-oriented mindset transforms challenges into opportunities and setbacks into lessons. Cultivating a strong, resilient mind allows you to navigate life's obstacles with clarity and purpose.

- **Know Your Intent:** Intent is the driving force behind every action. It's your "why." When your intentions are clear, your actions become purposeful, and your life gains direction. This principle reminds you to regularly check in with yourself to ensure that your actions align with your deeper goals and values.

- **Know Your Triggers:** Emotional triggers can derail even the best-laid plans. By identifying and understanding your triggers, you gain control over your responses. This awareness helps you respond thoughtfully rather than react impulsively. As a result, you can achieve more positive outcomes in your life.

These principles are the foundation of your journey. They are not just ideas to ponder; they are practices to live by. As you continue on your path, these principles will become your guideposts, helping you make decisions, overcome obstacles and grow into the person you are meant to be.

<u>YOUR OWN JOURNEY</u>

Your journey is unique. No one else can walk it for you, and no two paths are the same. This truth can be both liberating and daunting. The road ahead will be filled with moments of doubt, fear, and uncertainty. But it will also be filled with discovery, growth, and triumph. The key is to keep moving forward, even when the way is unclear.

Kiritin, from the story *Limits Unleashed*, faced similar uncertainties. He often felt lost, unsure of his direction, and overwhelmed by the challenges before him. But it was in those moments of doubt that his inner mentor, Kisan, would speak to him, offering guidance, wisdom, and encouragement. Like Kiritin, you too have an inner voice—a mentor within—that knows the way, even when you do not. Trust in it. Listen to it. It will lead you forward, even when the road ahead seems impossible.

As you journey, remember that setbacks are not failures but lessons. Each stumble is an opportunity to learn, to grow, and to recalibrate your course. The road ahead will test your commitment to the LIMIT Framework, but it is through these tests that you will truly come to embody its principles. Keep talking to your inner voice, keep practising the principles, and above all, keep going. The journey is long, but the rewards are immeasurable.

THE LASTING IMPACT OF KNOWING YOUR LIMITS

Knowing your limits is not about setting boundaries that hold you back; it's about understanding the landscape of your potential. When you know your limits, you gain the power to push beyond them, to challenge yourself, and to grow. This knowledge is what enables you to live authentically, to align your life with your true self, and to pursue what really matters to you.

The lasting impact of knowing your limits is profound. It transforms how you approach challenges, how you set goals, and how you measure success. It gives you the confidence to take risks, the wisdom to know when to step back, and the courage to keep moving forward. This impact is not just personal; it radiates outward, influencing those around you. When you live with clarity and purpose, you inspire others to do the same.

🤝 Action Step for Readers: Practice, Practice, Practice

The road ahead requires one thing above all else: practice. The LIMIT Framework is not a quick fix; it is a lifelong commitment. Practice is the key to mastering its principles, embedding them into your daily life, and ensuring that they guide you on your journey.

Start by choosing one principle of the LIMIT Framework that resonates with you. Perhaps you need to work on knowing your limits, or maybe you need to focus on aligning your actions with your interests. Whatever it is, make it a daily practice. Reflect on it, act on it, and let it shape your decisions.

As you grow more comfortable with one principle, move on to the next. Let each practice build upon the last, creating a strong foundation for the journey ahead.

Remember, the road ahead will not be easy. You will face setbacks, doubts, and fears. But if you stick with the LIMIT Framework, keep listening to your inner voice, and practice, practice, practice, you will find your way. The journey is not just about reaching a destination; it's about who you become along the way.

Your path is your own, and only you can walk it. Embrace the journey, trust in the process, and let the LIMIT Framework be your guide. The road ahead may be difficult, but it is also full of potential, growth, and fulfilment. Keep moving forward, and you will discover the true power of living a life aligned with your authentic self.

Readers' Notes:

Before You Go: A Personal Note

Dear Reader,

Thank you for dedicating your precious time to this book. Your journey through these pages reflects your deep commitment to personal growth and transformation, and I am truly grateful for your efforts. I hope that what you've discovered here resonates with you and adds value to your life's journey.

As we conclude the journey of *Limits Unleashed*, let's reflect on the key learnings and transformations we've encountered along the way. I invite you to take a moment to truly look inwards. Just as Kiritin was guided by Kisan, his inner mentor, I encourage you to **invoke** your own **inner guide**, **mentor**, or **friend**. This inner self is not just a concept—it's a powerful source of wisdom, strength, and clarity that resides within you. By connecting with this deeper part of yourself, you can find the answers to many of the questions that may have long been unanswered in your life.

What you witnessed in this book is just the spark that ignites the flame – a flame that will blaze through the darkness, revealing paths uncharted and possibilities untold. The journey you've embarked on is only in its infancy, with the most thrilling and transformative moments still lying ahead. What you've encountered is just the prelude to a world where limits are shattered and destinies are forged through perseverance and courage.

This is just the beginning. The true adventure is about to unfold. In the **sequel** to *Limits Unleashed*, you will witness the extraordinary transformation of Kiritin—once an average boy with no dreams, now someone who dares to chase the impossible.

Kiritin's journey takes an even more profound turn as he discovers the extraordinary within the ordinary. He faces a crucial decision: to follow a secure, traditional career path or to take a risk and pursue his passion for social entrepreneurship. Despite the fear of failure and the heavy weight of societal expectations, Kiritin chooses the path of uncertainty. This decision marks the culmination of his transformation. He quits his luxurious corporate life to mentor underprivileged youth, using the very principles that helped him overcome his own limitations. Through this journey, Kiritin transforms his life and ignites the potential in others, inspiring a new generation to believe in the power of possibility.

Prepare yourself for a story of courage, resilience, and the relentless pursuit of one's destiny. The journey continues, and I can't wait for you to join Kiritin in navigating the balance of risk and reward, passion and purpose. Together, we'll explore how even the most ordinary moments in life can lead to extraordinary transformations.

I would love to hear your thoughts, especially regarding the LIMIT Framework. Does it resonate with you? Do you think it could help you in fulfilling your life dreams or achieving what you truly desire? Your feedback is invaluable, and it would mean the world to me if you could share your reflections.

Please feel free to reach out with your feedback, questions, or to share your experiences. You can contact me directly at limitsunleashedbyak@gmail.com. I would be delighted to engage in a conversation with you and learn more about how this book has impacted your life.

Wishing you continued strength and fulfilment on your path forward.

Your well-wisher,

Alvin Kalicharan

Appendix

Decoding LIMIT Framework: The Essence of Each Character

Know Your LIMIT - "L" → Looking Inward

In the journey of personal growth and self-discovery, the first step in the "Know Your LIMIT" Framework is "L," which stands for **"Looking Inward"**. This critical practice involves focusing on what truly matters—understanding the difference between what you can control and what lies beyond your control. By mastering this distinction, you empower yourself to navigate life's challenges with greater clarity, resilience, and purpose.

Things You Can't Control

Life presents numerous elements that are outside your sphere of influence, including:

- **Your Birth:** The circumstances of your birth, including the time, place, and family into which you were born, are beyond your control.
- **Your Death:** While healthy living can influence longevity, the timing and circumstances of your death are not within your control.
- **Your Country:** The nation, culture, and political environment you were born into are predetermined.

- **Your Parents:** You cannot choose your parents, their values, or their influence on your early life.
- **Your Privilege (or Lack of):** Social and economic status, often influenced by factors like birthplace and family background, is not chosen by you.
- **Your Religion/Caste:** The religious and social structures you're born into shape your worldview but are inherited rather than chosen.
- **Other People's Actions, Thoughts, and Beliefs:** You cannot control others' behaviours, thoughts, or beliefs as these are personal to each individual.
- **The Exact Outcome of Anything:** While your actions can influence outcomes, the exact results are often affected by external factors beyond your control.

🔆 <u>Things You Can Control</u>

In contrast, certain aspects of life are within your control, primarily related to your internal world and personal decisions:

- **Expressing Gratitude:** You can choose to focus on the positive aspects of life and express thankfulness, enhancing mental well-being and relationships.
- **Your Actions:** You control the actions you take, which shape your life and its outcomes, even if you cannot control the exact results.
- **Your Thoughts:** You can train your mind to focus on constructive thoughts and challenge negative thinking patterns.
- **Your Mindset:** Adopting a growth mindset helps you see challenges as opportunities for learning and growth.

- **How You Spend Your Time:** You have the power to allocate your time according to your priorities, whether in work, relationships, hobbies, or self-care.
- **Where You Put Your Energy:** You can choose to invest energy in positive, productive activities rather than in draining, unproductive pursuits.
- **Who You Spend Time With:** Surrounding yourself with uplifting, supportive people is within your control and influences your thoughts and emotions.
- **Taking Care of Your Physical, Mental, and Emotional Needs:** Prioritising health through diet, exercise, rest, and self-care is entirely within your control.
- **Being Adaptable to Change:** While you can't control change, you can control how you respond to it, cultivating flexibility and resilience.
- **Not Getting Attached to an Outcome:** Focusing on the process rather than the result helps you stay grounded and reduce anxiety over things beyond your control.

Action Step for Readers: List the Things You Can vs. Can't Control

Looking Inward involves distinguishing between what is within your control and what is not. By creating a list of these things, you shift your focus from external factors to internal empowerment. This practice serves as a powerful reminder that while you can't control everything that happens in life, you can control your response to those events.

By embracing "Looking Inward," you direct your energy towards personal growth and fulfilment, making your journey through life more meaningful and balanced. In essence, the "L" in the LIMIT Framework is about embracing the power within you to influence your life positively, despite the many things that are beyond your control.

Readers' Notes:

Know Your LIMIT - "I" ➜ INTEREST

In the "Know Your LIMIT" Framework, the "I" stands for Your **Interest**, which is key to leading a fulfilling and joyful life. Understanding and identifying your interests goes beyond just recognising hobbies or pastimes; it's about discovering the passions that resonate deeply with you and can drive your purpose and career.

Identify Your Interest

To identify your interests, ask yourself: *What is one thing I could do for hours without getting bored or tired?* This question helps you pinpoint activities that truly captivate you, where you lose track of time and feel fully immersed. Whether it's writing, teaching, problem-solving, or creating art, your interests are the pursuits that bring you both joy and satisfaction.

What's Your Ikigai?

A profound way to identify your interests is through the concept of Ikigai, a Japanese philosophy that means "a reason for being." Ikigai lies at the intersection of four elements:

- **What you love (Your Passion):** Activities that excite and energise you.
- **What you are good at (Your Vocation):** Skills and talents that come naturally to you.
- **What the world needs (Your Mission):** Ways in which your interests and talents can positively impact others.
- **What you can be paid for (Your Profession):** Interests and skills that can be turned into a sustainable career.

By exploring these areas, you can find your Ikigai, aligning your interests with a meaningful and purposeful life. Living according to your Ikigai means not only pursuing your passions, but also contributing to the world in a fulfilling and rewarding way.

Why It's Important to Know Your Purpose

Knowing your purpose, revealed through your interests and Ikigai, is essential for several reasons:

- **Direction:** Your interests guide you towards activities and careers aligned with your true self, bringing clarity to your life.
- **Motivation:** Engaging in activities that resonate with your interests naturally boosts your motivation and energy.
- **Fulfilment:** Living according to your interests and purpose turns your daily routine into meaningful experiences.
- **Balance:** Harmonising your interests with your professional life reduces stress and enhances overall well-being.

Action Step for Readers: Consider What Comes Naturally to You

To identify your interests, reflect on:

- **What are you naturally good at?** Consider skills where you excel without much effort.
- **What do you love to do?** Think about activities that make you feel alive and engaged.
- **How can these interests contribute to the world?** Reflect on how your talents and passions can address a need or solve a problem.

By using the Ikigai framework to explore these questions, you can uncover your true interests and align them with a purposeful life. For more insights on discovering your Ikigai, explore the book *Ikigai: The Japanese Secret to a Long and Happy Life*. This book provides a deeper understanding of how to find and live your Ikigai, helping you align your interests with a life of purpose and joy.

Readers' Notes:

Know Your LIMIT - "M" ➔ MINDSET

In the "Know Your LIMIT" framework, the "M" stands for **Mindset**, underscoring the importance of understanding and controlling your thoughts. The mind is the command centre of your life, shaping how you perceive the world, respond to challenges, and interact with others. By mastering your mind, you can significantly enhance your mental well-being, resilience, and overall happiness.

Know and Control Your Mind

Your mind is constantly active, generating a stream of thoughts, emotions, and narratives—often referred to as the "monkey mind." This metaphor captures the restless and chaotic nature of our thoughts, which can jump from one idea to another, leading to anxiety or stress if left unchecked. Your internal dialogue, or self-talk, plays a crucial role in shaping your mindset and emotions. By becoming aware of this self-talk and guiding it positively, you gain control over your mental state.

Why It's Important

- **The Monkey Mind:** The "monkey mind" describes the restless, chattering thoughts that fill our minds. While it's natural for the mind to wander, unchecked mental chatter can lead to stress, anxiety, and negative thinking patterns. Recognising this aspect of your mind is the first step towards calming it and gaining control.
- **Neural Pathways:** Your brain operates like a network of pathways, where frequently travelled routes become stronger. This means that the more you practice a certain

way of thinking—whether positive or negative—the more your brain will default to that pattern. Consciously practicing positive thinking habits allows you to rewire your brain to become more resilient, optimistic, and focused.

- **Negativity Bias:** The brain has a natural tendency to focus on negative experiences more than positive ones, known as the "negativity bias." While this bias was useful for our ancestors in identifying threats, in modern life, it can lead to unnecessary worry and pessimism. By actively choosing to focus on positive thoughts and experiences, you can train your brain to appreciate the good things in life, counteracting the negativity bias and fostering a happier mindset.

- **Power of Words:** Simply labelling your emotions with words like "sad," "anxious," or "angry" can have a powerful calming effect on your mind. Naming an emotion activates the logical part of your brain, helping to regulate and reduce the intensity of the emotion. This technique not only manages current feelings but also contributes to long-term changes in how your brain responds to emotional stimuli.

What Can You Do?

- **Notice Your Mental Habits:** The first step to controlling your mind is awareness. Pay attention to your mental habits—whether they are fantasies, worries, or recurring thoughts. Developing an "Observing Self" allows you to step back and monitor these thoughts objectively, which is crucial for identifying unhelpful patterns and beginning the process of change.

- **Change Your Self-Talk:** Your self-talk significantly influences your mindset and emotions. If your self-talk is often negative or self-critical, you can deliberately change it to be more positive and supportive. For example, if you tend to dwell on your mistakes, practice telling yourself, "Mistakes are learning opportunities, and I am growing every day." Writing down the self-talk you want to adopt and repeating it in challenging situations can help internalise these positive messages.

- **Focus on Positive Experiences:** To counteract the brain's negativity bias, make a conscious effort to focus on positive experiences. When something good happens, whether it's a compliment, a pleasant moment, or a small success, take a few seconds to savour it. Holding onto these positive moments for at least five seconds helps strengthen the neural pathways associated with positivity, making it easier to notice and appreciate the good things in life.

- **Label Your Thoughts:** When you notice your mind spinning stories, worries, or fantasies, try labelling them with simple phrases like "Just thoughts" or "Thinking." This practice, derived from Zen meditation, helps you distance yourself from mental chatter, allowing you to see your thoughts more objectively. By doing so, you can take your thoughts less seriously, reducing their emotional impact and helping to calm your mind.

Action: Self-Talk

Your mind and body are deeply connected, and the way you talk to yourself influences your physical and emotional health. To harness the power of self-talk:

- **Find out what is on your mind:** Take time to reflect on your thoughts and recognise the recurring themes in your self-talk. Are they mostly positive, encouraging, and constructive, or do they lean towards negativity and self-criticism?
- **Figure out what you are saying to yourself:** Pay attention to the specific language and tone you use in your internal dialogue. Are you being kind to yourself, or do you often put yourself down?
- **Deliberately shift your self-talk:** Once you've identified negative patterns, consciously replace them with more positive, supportive messages. This may take practice, but over time, you'll notice a significant shift in your mindset and emotional well-being.

By understanding and controlling your mind, you gain the power to shape your reality. Positive self-talk, mindfulness, and intentional thinking habits can transform the way you experience life, leading to greater resilience, happiness and inner peace.

Know Your LIMIT - "I" ➜ INTENT

In the "Know Your LIMIT" framework, the "I" stands for **Intent**, focusing on understanding the deeper motivations behind your actions. Intent goes beyond setting and achieving goals; it delves into the underlying reasons—the "why"—that drive those goals. Understanding your intent provides clarity, purpose, and resilience, helping you live a life aligned with your true desires and values.

Know Your Intent by Asking "Why"

Intent is about more than just what you want to achieve; it's about why you want to achieve it. While goals provide structure and direction, they often lack the emotional depth needed for long-term fulfilment. Intent, on the other hand, taps into your core desires and aspirations, providing a guiding force that gives your life meaning and purpose.

However, as we navigate the demands of daily life, it's easy to lose sight of this purpose. Routine tasks can become monotonous, and overwhelming workloads can lead to stress and burnout. Reconnecting with your deeper intents can help you rediscover your purpose and even guide you to recognise when it's time to make a significant change.

The Difference Between Intent and Goals

- **Goals**: Goals are specific, task-oriented objectives that you set for yourself. They often come from the mind, focusing on achieving a tangible outcome, such as completing a project, earning a certain amount of money, or reaching a career milestone. Goals are typically short-term and result-driven, providing clear markers of success or failure. However, once a goal is achieved, the sense of fulfilment it brings can be fleeting, as the focus quickly shifts to the next objective.

- **Intents**: Intents, in contrast, are broader, more emotional, and come from the soul. They represent the underlying reasons behind your goals—the "why" that drives you to pursue them in the first place. While goals might be about the destination, intents are about the journey and the personal growth you experience along the way. An intent is like a seed filled with potential. When you plant this seed and allow it to be nurtured by the experiences, challenges, and opportunities of life, it gradually grows into something meaningful, such as a strong sense of purpose, fulfilment, and happiness.

Unlike goals, which often have a clear endpoint, intents are ongoing. They evolve with you, helping you find purpose in small, everyday actions and guiding your decisions over the long term. Knowing your intents makes it easier to express your desires authentically to yourself and others, fostering deeper connections in your relationships, enhancing your work satisfaction, and bringing more meaning to your daily activities.

The Importance of Knowing Your Intent

Understanding your intent is crucial because it aligns your actions with your true desires and values. When you are clear about your intents:

- **You Gain Clarity**: Knowing your intent helps you clarify what you really want from life. It allows you to distinguish between superficial desires and deeper aspirations that are truly meaningful to you.
- **You Find Purpose**: By connecting your daily activities to your deeper intents, you infuse your life with purpose.

Even mundane or challenging tasks can become more fulfilling when they are seen as part of a larger, meaningful journey.

- **You Become Resilient**: A strong sense of intent acts as a foundation that supports you through life's challenges. When faced with obstacles, knowing why you are doing something helps you stay focused and motivated, making it easier to overcome setbacks and continue moving forward.

- **You Foster Authenticity** : When you know your intents, you become more comfortable expressing your true desires to yourself, your loved ones, and your community. This authenticity strengthens your relationships, as people are drawn to your genuine passion and purpose.

 Action Step for Readers: Discover the "Why"

To truly connect with your intent, it's important to take time for introspection. Discovering your "Why" can be a powerful exercise in understanding what drives you at a deeper level. Here's how you can do it:

1. **Sit Comfortably and Breathe**: Begin by finding a quiet place where you can sit comfortably. Close your eyes and focus on your breathing. Inhale slowly, counting to three in your head: One, Two, Three. Then exhale slowly, counting to four: One, Two, Three, Four. Repeat this breathing exercise three times. This simple mindfulness practice helps you centre yourself, calm your mind, and prepare for deeper reflection.

2. **Ask Yourself: "What Do I Want?"** Once you are calm and focused, ask yourself the question, "What do I want?"

The first answer that comes to mind might be something material or superficial, like wanting money, success, or recognition. This is normal. But to discover your true intent, push yourself to go deeper. Ask why you want these things. What deeper desire or need is fulfilled by achieving this goal? For example, if you desire financial success, is it because you value security, freedom, or the ability to provide for your loved ones?

3. **Be Honest**: This exercise is for you, so be completely honest with yourself. There's no right or wrong answer, only what is true for you. The goal is to peel back the layers of your desires to reveal the core intent that drives your actions. This process might take time, and your answers may evolve as you reflect more deeply. The important thing is to approach this exercise with openness and curiosity.

By regularly reflecting on your intents and asking yourself "Why," you align your actions with your true purpose. This alignment not only brings greater fulfilment but also empowers you to live a more intentional, authentic life. As you become more aware of your intents, you'll find it easier to make decisions that resonate with your values, leading to greater happiness and resilience in the face of life's challenges.

Readers' Notes:

Know Your LIMIT - "T" ➜ Trigger

In the "Know Your LIMIT" framework, the "T" stands for **Trigger**, highlighting the importance of recognizing and managing emotional triggers. These triggers are stimuli—whether they are a person, place, situation, or specific word—that provoke intense emotional reactions, often rooted in unresolved emotions from past experiences. By identifying and effectively managing these triggers, you can maintain emotional stability and foster healthier responses to stressful situations.

The Nature of Triggers

Triggers evoke strong emotions because they are linked to past memories, traumas, or unresolved issues. For instance, a specific smell might remind you of a painful memory, or a particular tone of voice could evoke feelings of inadequacy or anger. These triggers bypass your conscious thought process and elicit an immediate emotional response, often leaving you feeling overwhelmed or out of control.

Common sources of triggers include:

- **Past Trauma:** Unresolved traumatic experiences can create hypersensitivity to certain stimuli.
- **Childhood Experiences:** Stressful experiences during the formative years can shape your emotional landscape and trigger responses in adulthood.
- **Stress and Fatigue:** When you're stressed or tired, your emotional resilience decreases, making you more susceptible to triggers.

The Importance of Recognising Triggers

Identifying your triggers is the first step in managing them. When you understand what sets off your emotional responses, you can anticipate and prepare for these moments, reducing the likelihood of being blindsided. This awareness enables you to make conscious choices about how to respond, rather than reacting impulsively.

Healthy Coping Strategies for Managing Triggers

Once you've identified your triggers, develop strategies to cope with them effectively:

- **Calling on Your Social Support:**

  - **Connection is Key:** Reaching out to someone you trust can provide comfort and perspective. Talking through your feelings can help diffuse the intensity of the emotional response.
  - **Action:** Identify a few trusted individuals you can reach out to when feeling triggered. Practice initiating conversations with them during less stressful times to make reaching out second nature when you're under emotional duress.
  - **Reflection:** After seeking support, reflect on whether sharing your feelings helped and how the other person's response impacted your emotional state.

- **Deep Breathing:**

  - **Reset Your Nervous System:** Engage in deep breathing exercises to calm the body and mind by activating the parasympathetic nervous system, which lowers your heart rate and reduces stress.

- ○ **Action:** Practice deep breathing regularly so that it becomes a habit. Use techniques like inhaling for four seconds, holding for four seconds, and exhaling for four seconds when you recognise a trigger.
- ○ **Reflection:** Reflect on how deep breathing influenced your emotional state and whether it gave you the pause needed to respond rather than react.

- **Exercising:**

  - ○ **Release the Tension:** Physical activity helps channel the energy that builds up when you're triggered, dissipating stress hormones and boosting mood-enhancing endorphins.
  - ○ **Action:** Develop a consistent exercise routine and engage in physical activity immediately when triggered.
  - ○ **Reflection:** After exercising, reflect on its impact on your emotions and track which types of exercise are most effective in managing triggers.

- **Expressive Writing:**

  - ○ **Process Your Emotions:** Writing about your feelings allows you to process them in a structured way, reducing the intensity of your response.
  - ○ **Action:** Keep a journal for expressive writing and write about your feelings when you experience a trigger.
  - ○ **Reflection:** Reflect on how writing influenced your emotions and review past entries to identify patterns in your triggers and responses.

- **Keeping a Journal:**

  - **Track Your Triggers:** Document your emotional responses over time to identify patterns and work towards resolving underlying issues.
  - **Action:** Make journaling a regular habit, documenting your triggers, emotional responses, and coping strategies.
  - **Reflection:** Regularly review your journal entries to reflect on any patterns or recurring triggers.

- **Mindfulness Meditation:**

  - **Stay Present:** Mindfulness practices encourage you to stay present and observe your thoughts and feelings without judgment, helping you respond more thoughtfully.
  - **Action:** Set aside time for mindfulness meditation daily and use mindfulness techniques when triggered.
  - **Reflection:** Reflect on whether mindfulness helped you stay centred during a triggering moment and how it changed your perception of the trigger.

Responding vs. Reacting

The key to managing triggers is learning to respond rather than react. Reacting is immediate and often driven by the emotional brain, leading to impulsive actions you might later regret. Responding involves taking a moment to process your emotions, consider your options, and choose a course of action that aligns with your values and goals.

By practising self-awareness and employing these coping strategies, you can transform your triggers from points of vulnerability into opportunities for growth. Over time, you'll find that you can navigate emotional challenges with greater ease, leading to a more balanced and fulfilling life. Understanding your emotional triggers and learning to manage them effectively empowers you to live a more emotionally resilient and controlled life.

Readers' Notes:

Practical Tips for Implementing the Framework

1. Leveraging the Power of Self-Awareness Exercise: Mindful Reflection on Personal Strengths and Weaknesses.

    - *Purpose:* To increase self-awareness and gain clarity on personal growth areas.
    - *How:* Set aside 15 minutes each day for a week to reflect on your recent actions, decisions, and emotional responses. Write down moments where you felt strong and aligned with your values, and moments where you felt challenged or unbalanced.
    - *Emotionally Engaging Tip:* As you reflect, visualise yourself as a tree, with your strengths being the roots that keep you grounded, and your weaknesses being the branches that can grow stronger with care and attention.

2. Investigating Your Core Values Exercise: The Values Deep Dive

    - *Purpose:* To identify and align your life with your core values.
    - *How:* Create a list of 10 values that are important to you. Then, narrow it down to the top 3 values that you feel are non-negotiable in your life. Reflect on

how these values are represented in your current daily actions and make a plan to integrate them more fully.

- *Emotionally Engaging Tip:* Imagine each of your top 3 values as a star in the night sky, guiding you like a North Star towards your true purpose.

3. Mindful Goal-Setting Exercise: The Vision Board

- *Purpose:* To visualise and commit to your goals with clarity.
- *How:* Gather images, quotes, and symbols that resonate with your goals and values. Arrange them on a board or digital platform. Place this board where you will see it daily.
- *Emotionally Engaging Tip:* Each time you look at your vision board, take a deep breath and imagine yourself stepping into the future it represents, feeling the joy and fulfilment of achieving your dreams.

4. Integrating Self-Compassion Exercise: The Loving-Kindness Practice

- *Purpose:* To foster self-compassion and kindness.
- *How:* Spend 5 minutes each day sending loving thoughts to yourself. Use phrases like, "May I be happy, may I be healthy, may I be at peace." Then, extend these wishes to others in your life.
- *Emotionally Engaging Tip:* As you practice, imagine a warm, golden light filling your heart and expanding outward, enveloping yourself and others in a blanket of love and compassion.

5. Transforming Challenges into Opportunities Exercise: The Resilience Journal

- *Purpose:* To build resilience by reframing challenges as opportunities for growth.
- *How:* Each time you face a challenge, write down the situation in your journal. Reflect on what you can learn from it and how it can make you stronger.
- *Emotionally Engaging Tip:* Visualise yourself as a warrior facing a dragon. Each challenge you conquer adds a new piece of armour, making you more resilient and ready for the next battle.

Mindfulness Practices and Techniques

1. Mindful Breathing Exercise: The 4-7-8 Breath

   - *Purpose:* To calm the mind and body.
   - *How:* Inhale for 4 counts, hold the breath for 7 counts, and exhale slowly for 8 counts. Repeat 5 times.
   - *Emotionally Engaging Tip: Imagine each breath as a wave washing over the shore, cleansing away stress and leaving behind a sense of peace.*

2. Body Scan Meditation Exercise: Progressive Muscle Relaxation

   - *Purpose:* To reduce physical tension and promote relaxation.
   - *How:* Starting from your toes, tense each muscle group for a few seconds, then release. Move up through your body, finishing with your face and scalp.
   - *Emotionally Engaging Tip:* As you release each muscle, imagine tension leaving your body like sand slipping through your fingers, grounding you in the present moment.

3. Mindful Walking Exercise: Walking Meditation

   - *Purpose:* To integrate mindfulness into everyday activities.

- *How:* Walk slowly and deliberately, focusing on the sensations in your feet, the rhythm of your breath, and the sights and sounds around you.
- *Emotionally Engaging Tip:* Picture yourself walking through a peaceful forest, each step connecting you more deeply with the earth and your inner self.

4. Mindful Eating Exercise: Savouring the Present Moment

- *Purpose:* To cultivate mindfulness during meals.
- *How:* Choose a meal or snack to eat mindfully. Pay attention to the colours, textures, smells, and flavours. Chew slowly and savour each bite.
- *Emotionally Engaging Tip:* Imagine each bite as a gift from nature, nourishing your body and soul. Feel the gratitude for the food and the moment.

5. Cultivating Gratitude Exercise: The Gratitude Jar

- *Purpose:* To shift focus from lack to abundance.
- *How:* Each day, write down something you are grateful for on a small piece of paper. Place it in a jar. When the jar is full, read through your notes.
- *Emotionally Engaging Tip:* Visualise each note as a seed of happiness planted in the garden of your heart. Watch your garden grow as you nurture it with gratitude.

6. Loving-Kindness Meditation Exercise: Extending Compassion

- *Purpose:* To foster a sense of connection and kindness.
- *How:* Start with yourself and repeat, "May I be happy, may I be healthy, may I be safe." Gradually extend

these wishes to loved ones, acquaintances, and even those with whom you have conflicts.

- *Emotionally Engaging Tip:* Imagine sending out rays of warm, golden light to each person as you repeat the phrases, strengthening the bonds of compassion that connect us all.

7. Mindful Observation Exercise: Noticing the Little Things

- *Purpose:* To cultivate present-moment awareness.
- *How:* Choose an object in your environment and spend 5 minutes observing it. Notice its details, colours, shapes, and textures.
- *Emotionally Engaging Tip:* Imagine seeing the object for the first time, like a child filled with wonder. Let it remind you of the beauty in everyday life.

8. Mindful Listening Exercise: Deep Listening

- *Purpose:* To improve communication and connection.
- *How:* When someone speaks to you, focus entirely on their words without planning your response. Listen with your heart as well as your ears.
- *Emotionally Engaging Tip:* Picture yourself as a calm lake, reflecting the other person's words without judgment or interruption. Let your stillness invite deeper connection.

9. Visualization Meditation Exercise: The Safe Place

- *Purpose:* To create a mental refuge from stress.
- *How:* Close your eyes and imagine a place where you feel completely safe and at peace. It could be a real location or one you create in your mind.

Spend a few minutes exploring this place in your imagination.

- *Emotionally Engaging Tip:* As you visualise, feel the sense of safety and peace wash over you, like a protective bubble shielding you from the chaos of the outside world.

10. Guided Imagery Exercise: The Mountain Meditation

- *Purpose:* To cultivate stability and strength.
- *How:* Imagine yourself as a mountain, unshaken by the changing weather around you—calm, grounded, and enduring.
- *Emotionally Engaging Tip:* As you embody the mountain, feel the power and stability within you grow, anchoring you firmly in the face of life's challenges.

Resources for Further Reading

Below are some carefully curated resources for further exploration, linked to the key themes and topics discussed in the book:

1. Understanding and Implementing the LIMIT Framework

   - *"Atomic Habits" by James Clear:* This book delves into how small changes can lead to significant transformations, much like the LIMIT Framework's emphasis on gradual improvement and mastery. Clear's approach to habit formation is highly actionable and aligns with the practical steps discussed in the story.

   - *"The Power of Now" by Eckhart Tolle:* Tolle's teachings on presence and mindfulness are essential to the "Interest" and "Time" elements of the LIMIT Framework, helping readers stay grounded in the present moment while pursuing their goals.

   - *"Mindset: The New Psychology of Success" by Carol S. Dweck:* Dweck's exploration of fixed vs. growth mindsets ties in directly with the "Limitations" aspect of the LIMIT Framework, offering insights into how changing your mindset can help you overcome barriers and unleash your full potential.

2. Mindfulness Practices and Techniques

- *"Wherever You Go, There You Are" by Jon Kabat-Zinn:* A foundational text on mindfulness, this book provides practical exercises and reflections that are perfect for integrating into daily life, echoing the mindfulness practices recommended in the story.

- *"The Miracle of Mindfulness" by Thich Nhat Hanh:* This book offers simple yet profound exercises in mindfulness that resonate with the techniques described in "Limit Unleashed," particularly around being present and cultivating a calm, focused mind.

- *"The Headspace Guide to Meditation and Mindfulness" by Andy Puddicombe:* Puddicombe's approach is accessible and practical, making it a great resource for beginners looking to implement mindfulness into their routine, much like the readers following the LIMIT Framework.

3. Exploring Purpose and Passion (Interest)

- *"Ikigai: The Japanese Secret to a Long and Happy Life" by Héctor García and Francesc Miralles:* This book explores the concept of Ikigai, or finding one's reason for being, which is deeply connected to the "Interest" aspect of the LIMIT Framework. It provides insights into aligning your passions with your daily life.

- *"Drive: The Surprising Truth About What Motivates Us" by Daniel H. Pink:* Pink's book delves into the intrinsic motivations that fuel our passions, aligning well with the concept of discovering and nurturing your true interests as discussed in the story.

4. Wisdom from the Bhagavad Gita

    - *"The Essence of the Bhagavad Gita: Explained by Paramhansa Yogananda" by Swami Kriyananda:* This book breaks down the teachings of the Gita in a way that is relatable and actionable, particularly in the context of mastering the mind and understanding one's purpose—key themes in "Limit Unleashed."
    - *"The Bhagavad Gita: A New Translation" by Stephen Mitchell:* For readers looking to dive deeper into the philosophical underpinnings that inspire the LIMIT Framework, Mitchell's translation offers accessible yet profound insights into the timeless wisdom of the Bhagavad Gita.

5. Overcoming Obstacles and Limiting Beliefs

    - *"The Obstacle Is the Way: The Timeless Art of Turning Trials into Triumph" by Ryan Holiday:* Holiday's book is a modern take on ancient Stoic philosophy, offering practical advice on how to turn challenges into opportunities—a concept that resonates with the "Limitations" aspect of the LIMIT Framework.
    - *"Grit: The Power of Passion and Perseverance" by Angela Duckworth:* Duckworth's research on grit and perseverance complements the story's theme of pushing past limitations to achieve long-term success and fulfilment.

6. Time Management and Productivity

    - *"Getting Things Done: The Art of Stress-Free Productivity" by David Allen:* Allen's methodology for managing tasks and projects aligns with the "Time" aspect of the LIMIT Framework, providing tools for organising your life in a way that reduces stress and increases efficiency.

- *"Deep Work: Rules for Focused Success in a Distracted World" by Cal Newport:* Newport's focus on deep, uninterrupted work ties directly into the story's emphasis on using time effectively and cultivating the focus necessary to pursue your true passions.

These resources will deepen your understanding of the concepts discussed in "Limit Unleashed," providing practical tools and insights to help you implement the LIMIT Framework in your own life, enhance mindfulness, and align with your true purpose.

The End